The Salt of the Earth

To Vivienne & John

Best Wishes

Dorothy G :

Georgina ('Ma') wearing a new dress bought for her by her brother John to celebrate Queen Victoria's diamond jubilee in 1897.

The Salt of the Earth

The diary of a poor family in Woodstock, 1900

Dorothy Calcutt

The Wychwood Press

Published in 1999 by
The Wychwood Press, an imprint of Jon Carpenter Publishing
2, The Spendlove Centre, Charlbury, Oxfordshire OX7 3PQ
Tel/fax 01608 811969

ISBN 1 902279 06 9

Printed in England by J. W. Arrowsmith Ltd., Bristol
Cover printed by KMS Litho, Hook Norton

Contents

Acknowledgements

I would like to thank my son-in-law Richard Owen for putting the book onto a computer, without which this book would never have been completed.

Also John and Richard Banbury, Mrs Rosemary Giraud, Mr Freeman, Mr Dennis Howes, Mrs Morris and Mrs Marion Rawlings for supplying photographs; Mrs Margaret Stringer (née Mansell) for details of the chair; and John Bruker, headmaster of Woodstock Primary School, who initiated the book.

Preface

I have spent most of my life either bringing up my children or teaching. My teaching life was mostly spent as an assistant at Woodstock Primary School.

Several times during my years there, some classes would have 'Victorian Times' as their class topic. One day the headmaster suggested that I encouraged my mother to come to school to talk to the children and answer questions. She had recently been widowed and so welcomed the opportunity as a relief from monotony. She was then about seventy-six years old. She had lived in Woodstock so she remembered the changing times, but more than this she recalled her family history. Some of this I already knew but some came as quite a shock to me. I was so engrossed in the topic that I wrote a short play that the children enjoyed acting.

My colleagues goaded me into recording the history, hoping one day it would be a good teaching aid. After returning from those trips to the school my mother would talk for hours recalling the past, only too pleased that ears were willing to listen.

I was born in 1920 and by that time medicine and education had progressed — but farming had nearly stood still. Binders, pulled by teams of horses, had replaced the scythes but otherwise things were much as they had been at the turn of the century. Mains water and electricity did not arrive in the small village of Coombe (spelt Combe after 1935) until the mid-thirties, so some of the episodes are very real to me.

There was much unemployment but no dole. Life expectancy was very short but even if you did grow old there was no pension. There was very little security of work because tied cottages ensured that you worked long hours for little pay — or moved on.

Although times were hard people lived each day as it came. Their faith in the United Methodist Chapel was rock solid. They suffered no stress. They were in fact very happy, singing or whistling the day through.

'Blessed is he that expecteth nothing, for he shall not be disappointed,' was often repeated. A few selfish men did spend money on beer they could ill afford and their families suffered accordingly.

Families were much larger but death came more frequently and they accepted their lot.

I hope you will enjoy my mother's reminiscences, recalling those 'good old days'.

Dorothy Calcutt

The Salt of the Earth

The family

Ma – Georgina, mother of a large family in extreme circumstances. She was very anxious that neighbours should know just how well they were doing.

Dad – George, her husband, a farm labourer who alternated between heavy drinking and going on the waggon.

Queenie, 22

Joe, 21

Charlie, 19

George, 17

Tom, 15

Betty, 12

Sarah, 11

Sid, 9

Dora, 6

Jackie, 4

Uncle John

A winter's struggle

The cock was crowing in the distance. He thought that just another day was dawning. The guinea fowl began to chatter; they were ignorant of the true facts too. Much nearer to Georgina were the eldest and youngest of her offspring. The eldest, still sleeping in her bedroom, was snoring so violently that Georgie wondered how anyone could still be asleep. The youngest – Jackie – still slept in a cot very close to her side, but during the past month he had developed a very worrying cough. He was coughing now, although he appeared to be asleep. Next to her, however, lay her husband George – he worked hard and she respected him for it; but how he could sleep through this assortment of noises she could never understand. She could feel the rise and fall of the old patchwork quilt, so his rest was undisturbed.

Georgie, however, was excited. She had woken early, feeling that, today, good news at last would come her way. It was the first of January 1900 – a new year and a new century too. Only two months ago a travelling gypsy had assured Georgie that the turn of the century would be the turn of her luck. The gypsy had been so positive that Georgie was completely convinced. Thinking about this prediction had kept her mind from the stark realities of life.

George, however, was blunt – 'You shouldn't listen to them diddikais. No truth in any of their rubbish,' was his comment. But she had listened. She needed some fantasy to help her through each day and night. Now that fantasy had been fostered and cultivated until it was reality; it had kept her awake last night and it had woken her early today. This reality was shared by no one. She had attempted to get Queenie to understand, but Queenie's whole life was taken up with the Methodist chapel and in no uncertain terms she had told her mother that prayer was the only way to get help. Queenie openly prayed that her mother would turn a deaf ear to the gypsies.

Georgie lay there, musing; she was wide awake now and what better way to start the century than to 'count one's blessings'? Of this she was

Dad, with one of his pups just in the picture.

sure Queenie would approve – indeed she sang it continuously.

For most of her life Queenie had been a burden and she knew it, but although Georgie would not admit it – maybe she didn't even realise it – she had during the past months found encouragement in Queenie's simple rock-based character. Early in life she had suffered from epileptic fits and was not expected to live, hence the fact she still slept in her parents' bedroom, but although she appeared to have outgrown this affliction she was left with very little eyesight. She was completely blind in her right eye and the left was covered with a membrane apart from one small speck. This usable part was perfect but the range was very restricted. She could read very well indeed but the book had to be placed just a few inches from her left ear. This was a severe handicap – indeed when she walked she always had to face the right. During her life she had been at times ridiculed, at times protected and at times hidden, but these limitations had strengthened and hardened her character. Her pleasures had been non-existent but her life so simple and narrow that as yet she felt neither deprived nor bitter.

She was approaching her twenty-third birthday now and was the eldest of ten. She had never been a financial help to the family but she was 'a mother's blessing'.

Father could see that no man would ever be attracted to her. She didn't mind: she didn't value charm anyway. She had never even seen herself in a mirror so her toilet, such as it was, did not have the objective of improving things. Clothes were very necessary but, if she had listed her priorities, not important. Her hand stitching was superb, it was indescribably neat and strong, rows and rows of pintucks encircling the hems of all the petticoats and pinafores needed in such a family. Every garment brought home from 'service' and discarded by the rest of the family found its way to Queenie. It might get transformed from 'milady's old coat' to trousers for a small brother but that was something tangible, something which gave Queenie a satisfaction she so desperately needed. The leftover scraps of cottons were cut into identical squares and added to the next quilt. The tweeds were cut into identical finger-shaped pieces and pegged into the next rug.

Georgie was still reflecting on the past when she heard old Bill outside – buckets were rattling. He called every morning on all the households that could afford him, especially those without gardens. His job dictated that it should be finished before the rest of the world was awake. He didn't, of course, call at this cottage. Georgie disentangled herself from the pile of discarded garments that had been covered by the patchwork quilt. One by one she put on every garment she had worn the previous day – indeed a few of them had not been taken off. She did look, discreetly, at the last apron to see if she should 'turn it over' today, but decided against it. She gave Queenie a little shake, which she knew would produce the desired effect. Queenie was accustomed to dressing without showing bare patches of body, leg or even arm. She was expert by now but she need not have worried, Dad was just as proficient in pretending to be asleep. She tiptoed through the door – feeling each accustomed location – across the landing where Tom and Joe were sleeping and down the twisty stone stairs. Her twilight life enabled her to accomplish this with comparative ease.

Ma had already donned a 'coarse apron' Queenie had made from hessian. It had really been an old potato sack but did well for scrubbing the flagged floor or black-leading the grate. She was busy riddling the grate and a light wood ash was dancing over the flames of two candles standing on the table. 'Take that jug of water and thaw out the pump, Queenie,' said Mum. 'It's very cold this morning.'

A box of wood, neatly graded by size, had been placed under the table the previous evening, so in five minutes or less the flames were reaching

Strong's 'Cheap boot and shoe warehouse'.

up the chimney, rendering it unnecessary to light the oil lamp. A black kettle was already hanging on the hook.

Ma was eking out the porridge oats into a black cast-iron saucepan; after adding plenty of water she placed it on the hob, where it would stay until all the family had breakfasted. Just as Queenie returned, complaining about the severity of the frost, Dad appeared at the other doorway. He made a hasty departure to the bottom of the garden, braces dangling around his hips and the thongs in his boots trying to get free. But he made it as always, returning to complete his 'trappings'.

His strength was too great this morning, however, and as he pulled his thong, it snapped in his hand. 'Get young Dora to run up to Strong's for some new ones before she goes to school,' ordered Dad. Now Dora was a very willing six-year-old but recently Ma had cured a couple of wild rabbit skins and, together with snippets of thrown-out leather Tom had collected at the glove factory, she had made herself a new muff. Any chance to wear this would not be missed; unlike most new clothes, it was not intended for Sundays only. She would need a penny however and that could be ill spared today; it had already been allocated to the baker.

Dad swallowed a whole mug of sweet, black tea so fast that his hardened throat did not even recognise it was boiling hot. He replaced the white enamel mug on the table with a bang, tied a red spotted kerchief around his neck, put a grubby, greasy cap on his head and was off to give his horses their nosebags.

During this time Ma had stood 'twixt table and fire plaiting her long hair. Her hands were adept at twisting it into a fascinating shape at the back of her head, two combs were placed in the front to tidy up the wisps and dozens of hairpins were pushed in like clockwork. She didn't even notice or care that hairdressing should not take place over food – it was a necessary job and she was in the necessary place to control the fire, the porridge and the tea. Queenie had already been sent to the washhouse again with a bundle of kindling wood to light the fire under the copper. It was Monday, so in spite of the new year, the severity of the weather and the interruptions of coughing, the washing just had to be done.

Next to descend the stairs was Joe, followed closely by Dora. Without either tea or porridge, she was sent with one penny but without even one grumble to rouse the Strong household for one pair of thongs.

'Have you put on your clean socks, Joe?' inquired Ma. 'You bet I have,' he retorted. 'Last week's pair were so thin and threadbare, but these are so darned they are as thick as two pair – just right for a day like this.' Joe was always grateful. He would be twenty-two this year so now he could 'do as he liked'. He had a kind, gentle nature but combined with this was strength and determination. He worked hard at Blenheim Palace in the gardens, he spent hours on his allotment, he was quite a good self-taught musician, he had a superb bass voice which had been developed at the United Methodist Chapel – but he had 'signed the pledge' and he was continually trying to convert others, most of all his father.

'Only porridge today, Joe, and no milk at all,' from his mother. 'That's alright Mum,' he answered. 'There are many in the world today with no breakfast at all.' Coughing punctuated the conversation and the word 'doctor' loomed up in Ma's mind, but she dismissed it again just as quickly because she knew she did not have the wherewithal to pay him. What had happened to the gypsy's prophecy?

The front door was flung open and in rushed Dora carrying a swede. It was huge and perfect and a deep purple colour. Dora stroked it. 'Isn't it a beauty, Ma? I found it just outside the gate. It must have fallen from Sam's cart; we can keep it, can't we?' she pleaded.

'Yes of course we can,' said Ma with a wry smile. 'I expect Sam allowed it to fall there purposely. That's his first good deed in the twentieth century; we'll have stew for dinner with those bones and that swede.'

But secretly she thought the gypsy was responsible.

It was now a quarter past seven and Tom had just dragged himself down – he always needed help in the morning. He was fifteen and had had three years training as a glove cutter. His apprenticeship was over now and today was to be his first day working completely unaided. He was only in the room a few minutes, both brothers leaving together. Joe was whistling 'Onward Christian Soldiers' but Tom was in no such happy mood at this early hour.

Dad was soon back for his 'nosebag'. 'My, those 'orses were frisky this morning, I reckon we are in for a fall of snow – I've just seen a skein of geese heading south too. Much too high for the gun though, we could have done with one of those this week.'

The coughing continued and this time Ma voiced her thoughts aloud. 'We really should have the doctor, but I'll never find the money till summer and he'll either be better or gone before then.'

'Take no thought for the morrow, that's what the good book says,' interrupted Queenie. 'Matthew 6:34. Everyone ought to know that chapter; the preacher used it for his text last week.'

Dad made no comment. These decisions were no concern of his; making the money go round was no concern of his either. He ate his porridge in huge mouthfuls, it was piled high with brown (pieces) sugar but his mind was occupied by the fact that rats had actually gnawed through the horses' nosebags during the night and now he would have to repair them. So when he picked up his red dinner kerchief, which contained the top of a cottage loaf, a lump of cheese and an onion, he gave no opinion about the necessity of a doctor's visit for Jackie. He ignored the question because, his mind being so preoccupied, he had not in fact registered it.

'So long Georgie,' he said, giving her a quick peck of a kiss. 'I shall stay up the top field till we've done three quarters of an acre – that's enough for two 'orses in one day. When I get back to the farm, I shall muck out the stables and bed 'em down well. I'm going to set a few gin traps; there's too many rats eating them 'orses oats.' He was gone.

Ma lifted the lid from the porridge pot, conscientiously counting the number of breakfasts that still had to come out of it. 'Hurry up you other four. Jackie will not be going to school today, he is coughing too much.'

The meagre porridge was supplemented by a cup of cocoa made wholly with water straight from the black kettle. Liberal helpings of sugar were added and all the children were satisfied because they at least all thought they had had a good breakfast.

There were grumbles from nine-year-old Sid because he hated school and would suggest any excuse for not going. The twins next door went on alternate days because they shared a pair of boots, so he was trying to lend his boots to any one of his sisters. It was no use, however. Mum insisted that the law said you had to go and if you stayed at home the inspector would be after her.

For Betty, however, the situation was different – she would be twelve years old this week so next week she would be ready to earn her own living. She pleaded with her mother to go to one of the glove factories but Mum's mind had been made up even before any of her girls were born.

'No girl of mine will ever go there,' she insisted. 'What sort of a wife will you make if you get no training in housework and cooking? We don't have room for you to sleep any longer, so it's service for you and that's that. Those factory girls swear worse than the men do. I've brought you up to be honest and 'ardworking. That factory is no good for you.'

Betty persevered – she wanted a good time, no living like Joe for her,

Woodstock School and railway station.

digging his allotment, singing hymns all day, joining Band of Hope and signing the pledge. Oh, no, that wasn't her idea of life. But mother's oft repeated phrase that settled all arguments was so tested and proven and so final that the younger ones dreaded it. 'You can do as you like when you are twenty-one, young lady. Now off to school the lot of you and mind you walk in the middle of the road!' And to Queenie: 'Fetch in the washing tray and let's get started.'

The last spoonful of porridge was taken up to Jackie.

Ma piled the dirty enamelware into a similar bowl – spread a piece of valuable newspaper over the scrubbed deal table and the oval washing tray was put on that. A galvanised bucket was used to carry the boiling water from copper to tray. A large lump of white soap was cut from a long stick and after rolling up sleeves she and Queenie started rubbing and scrubbing. 'I want it all done by eleven, if possible. Then I shall have time to get the dinner.' 'Let's sing 'Onward Christian Soldiers',' proposed Queenie. 'It makes us rub more quickly.' So through all the verses and endless choruses they sang, till there was an unexpected knock at the door. Queenie opened it and announced the postman.

'Will you take this telegram up to North Lodge, Queenie? You'll get a penny if you do.' Queenie's face lit up – she liked a walk through the park. She knew every inch of the way to North Lodge so without any hesitation she fetched a buttonhook and her boots. They were quickly buttoned up – you didn't need eyes for that. She put on her hat and pushed through a hatpin to secure it. 'That will be one more penny towards my new boots,' she said with pride and out she went. Although the persistent cough was still uppermost in Ma's thoughts she attributed this windfall to the gypsy again.

Ma had almost finished the washing when Queenie returned – much of it was blowing stiff on the line in the garden. The black pot on the hob varied from a gentle simmer to a rolling boil according to the ferocity of the flaming sticks. It was filled with bones; the promised swede and dumplings that she knew would meet with approval. 'I'm glad you're home in time, Queenie,' said Ma. 'We'll sit down together and have some stew before the children come in.'

At that moment there came a firm knock on the door and the baker's lad pushed his way in carrying a large square breadbasket. He called 'Baker!' at the top of his voice as if he expected the room to be empty.

'I'm afraid I've only got tuppence for bread today,' apologised mother. She had a guilty feeling ever since she had allowed that penny to go on Dad's thongs. The lad made a quick, snap answer. 'In that case you can have one new loaf or two of last Saturday's.'

'Oh good, it must be two stale ones then please,' replied Ma. He put two large cottage loaves on the table and was gone.

'I was right again,' said Queenie. 'I said take no thought for the morrow. We've enough for today now – my prayers have been answered.'

Mother smiled but kept her secret to herself. She was already planning the meals for the rest of the day. She still had some of the charity coal left from Christmas, so she could use a little today, firstly to heat the oven for a bread pudding, and secondly to heat the flat irons so she could make a start on the ironing immediately. Then when the children returned from afternoon school she would allow them to make toast. They could use some of Dad's honey – he loved keeping his bees – or as a very special treat today, they could enjoy some beef dripping. The neighbour's lad who worked at The Bear was often given some. Neighbours were neighbours in the true sense of the word, the less you had the more you shared what you did have.

The children ran in for their midday meal, taking off a few of their outdoor clothes and piling them in a corner of the room.

'There's lovely stew,' said mother as she busied herself ladling it onto the enamel plates, placing them on the newspaper-covered table. Comments of approval came from all of them. 'You are as good a cook as Mrs Beeton,' was the praise from Betty and mother seized her chance to push home her point. 'I was properly trained in service, young lady. Of course, that's why it is so good.'

'More, please! More please! I finished first,' shouted Sid. 'You would,' commented Ma. 'You're good at eating even if you are not much use at school.'

The usually quiet, thoughtful Sarah at last voiced her ideas on moral standards. 'When I leave school next year, Ma, I'll do whatever you want me to. I'll listen to William Booth, I'll sign the pledge and I won't marry anyone who hasn't signed the pledge either.'

'I'm glad you're making up your mind so soon,' responded Ma, 'but time goes so quickly – hurry up back to school. Did you have the stick this morning, Sid?'

'Only once,' he bragged as he ran out of the doorway.

The moment they had gone Ma tied a piece of string across the room from beam to beam, so convenient for hanging anything that needed airing. It was put there every Monday and stayed until Saturday evening. This had the effect of making the room appear darker and smaller. It was only about nine feet by ten and the centre was taken up by a table three feet by four. The window frame was very small too and it was divided into sixteen leaded panes; that would have ensured a dark room anyway but, to make doubly sure that no one peeped in, a net curtain was draped over all and a couple of leggy geraniums did their utmost to survive. A very strong box, a relic of Ma's service days, stood on the window seat: it now housed the vital darning and patching equipment. On this box stood a pot of Mind-your-own-business. The way it snuggled to the pot and tumbled down the sides, 'like mother's jam-making pot boiling over,' always fascinated Dora. Dad, however, likened it to froth when the landlord had overfilled a pint pot. The ceiling was low – a mere seven feet in the highest parts but not even six where the oak beams crossed above. This made it inevitable that the adults could not stand completely erect, but the addition of long pants, combinations and chemises on the line made crossing the room more like walking under the bunting at the jubilee. The ceiling was whitewashed every year but it quickly deteriorated to a toned yellow again, created by the smoking fire and the damp steam that clung daily from the washing up bowl, but was much more noticeable on Mondays.

The floor in this room was flagged but there were several pegged rugs, the largest being placed in front of the fire. Ma did have a new one, which was used on Sundays only, that had already been rolled up and placed under her bed. These rugs were the heaviest, dustiest floor covering ever invented, but they were warm. The children sat on them, as often there were not enough chairs or vacant places at table for everyone. During the summer months this was solved by sending the children out to play whilst adults ate. The door opened directly onto the road; it had no doormat but, as a substitute, it had a large tightly woven sack printed in large letters 'Hudson & Co. To be returned.' It was pushed against the door in the evenings in an attempt to filter at least some of the draught.

The combination of dust, smoke and steam in such a small area produced an undesirable atmosphere. You only needed the smell of boiling bacon, or bubble and squeak in the frying pan, to complete this homely climate. This was what the children had been born into, mother sitting in a wicker chair suckling the latest addition to the family – both babe and mother enveloped in yards of pin-tucked flannel petticoats.

This was the security of home and very few visitors ever crossed the threshold – except sometimes the local preacher on Sunday. Mother wished this security and satisfaction could continue indefinitely, but the wicked outside world had to be faced and she honestly thought the best way of attacking these evils was to keep the children in complete ignorance for as long as possible.

Sunday was different; the airing clothes could not be there on Sundays. Although Dad seldom if ever went to chapel now, he still insisted that no work be done on Sundays. Animals had to be fed but that was the limit. He never took his gun out as he counted that as pleasure. He would train his family right – he was even more strict than Joe on this point. The Bible was the only permitted literature, hymns the only permitted music. The children spent most of the day going to and from the chapel, sitting on hard benches. This was no hardship: everyone did it. 'Our fathers built the chapel, so we are very lucky to be able to use it.' The children knew how to sit still, or perhaps swing their legs because they wouldn't reach the floor (a good slap on the knee stopped it for at least a few minutes).

Dora loved to go with Queenie, whose first request was, 'What are the hymn numbers?' as she could not see that distance. Dora read out the numbers in a reverential whisper while Queenie shouted back each hymn correctly. Dora thought she was clever but Betty felt embarrassed and wished she didn't have to endure it. Worse was to follow, however. Queenie was wide awake listening for the text of the sermon. The very moment the local preacher had announced the book chapter and verse, in her loudest voice she would announce the text before the preacher could open his mouth. Dora felt like giving her a pat on the back but Betty would have preferred something much harder in a different place.

So it was that Betty was starting out in life, to see the pleasures and greed of the rich, because that was how life would exhibit itself to her. Until now there were just two ways of living, good and bad. There was no such thing as a white lie – that was wickedness – and as William Booth was preaching, one social drink was the beginning of the end.

You accepted your station and did not 'covet' others. Indeed Mrs Alexander's new hymn had been written with this purpose in mind.

The rich man in his castle
The poor man at his gate
He made them high or lowly
And ordered their estate.

They sang and re-sang it until they knew it was true and didn't even get a chance to doubt it.

Ma's one worry at the moment was that Betty would 'grow up' before going into service. It was much better that she went into the world in complete ignorance. Then she could pick up all the necessary knowledge as she grew up. That was the way she had grown up – that was the way that all animals grew up, and that was what she wanted for her daughters. If she relented and allowed Betty to go to the glove factory, her firm ideals of family upbringing would be undermined and shattered, probably in the first twenty-four hours.

So it was that she started the fundamental chores of every Monday afternoon. Much starching to be done first, every collar, pinafore and tablecloth. When those articles were tightly rolled she collected all the Sunday clothes, brushed them thoroughly, folded them, then returned them upstairs to lie in a large drawer until next Sunday. They had no wardrobe; indeed there was no room for one.

By now the flat irons were hot, so an old blanket was put on the table and folded pieces of sheet on top. Using a special iron holder made by Dora, she picked up one flat iron from the trivet. She turned it upside down and spat on it – yes it sizzled, so it was very hot – hot enough for any 'whites' that were ready.

Jackie was still coughing upstairs and Ma's mind was toying with the idea of spending her last ha'penny on black jack for him. She had prick-seamed four pairs of gloves this week, tomorrow they would be collected and paid for. They would produce the sum of one shilling and fourpence. So it was that just as the persistent coughs had weighed in favour of spending the ha'penny, that the noisy healthy part of the family could be heard coming from school.

As always the willing Dora was nominated to 'slip up to Turrills' for one ha'penny-worth of blackjack.' She was dependable. She could be trusted to walk into the middle of the road where at least the mud was less deep.

'Have any of you seen the postman today?' questioned Ma.

'Yes,' answered Queenie 'He's already been by three times, but he didn't have one for us. Are you expecting one from George and Charlie?'

'Not really, but I'm dreading the arrival of that letter from Canada that Joe is expecting.'

George and Charlie were her other two sons, aged 17 and 19 respectively. They had left last year having no work and no likelihood of any. Uncle John (Ma's only brother) had offered to walk with them to the Fens. He had been on a similar excursion a few years earlier when men were needed to dig railway cuttings. This time they would be digging ditches to drain the fens. Work was plentiful there. They arranged to stay about six months or a year then return, hopefully quite rich.

Uncle John was a bachelor, the tallest man for miles around. Everyone looked up to him in every way. His hairstyle was unique. He went to the barber weekly and had his hair on both head and chin cut off all over as short as it could be with scissors. He never shaved, but he always looked as if he needed one – maybe it was intended as a rebuff to any forthcoming girl friends. There were many offers but they were all treated like stone. He was in the habit of wearing corduroy trousers, tied just under the knee. Tucked into the knot was a small scraper, which was used for countless jobs – cleaning shoes, hoes etc. These, as all his clothes, had to be made to measure – every one else could manage with cast offs, but not him.

John knew that he was different, he had grown up with this knowledge. Every week when he had called at the coaching inn there was money waiting for him from a faraway bank. If he missed one week there were two lots there the next, so when he was away at work for six months or more it had built up to a considerable sum. He was in fact quite a rich man. How long this had been going on, or why, he had no idea. He only knew he or his mother had been collecting it ever since he could remember.

One other annual event was a puzzle to him. It had been going on since as far back as he could remember. He was invited to an inn in Witney and, after being given a meal by an unknown benefactor, he was taken first to the best tailor for new clothes of very superior quality, then to a seamstress for similar shirts, then to the cordwainery to be measured for boots. He was always the best-dressed man in town. Everyone admired his strength

Ma's brother John relaxing on the wall outside his house in Freeland, with a friend.

and stature but not his feet. If a pair of boots could have been purchased to fit him, they would have been approximately size 15 or 16. They were always made of very strong horsehide, which tended to make them appear even larger. They were ridiculed by all. You either fell over them or climbed a ladder to get over them or made a detour round them, but they were strong, they were waterproof and never ever shabby. Dora, who had difficulty lifting them, was always willing to polish them for 'a bottle of pop'. John did not drink alcohol – in his youth he had been so embarrassed by his size that he hated social company – but this new 'pop' he enjoyed. So, whenever he was at his sisters, a crate of pop was brought: it was John's, he paid for it, but he was quite liberal with it if you had favoured him in any way. The children loved pushing in the glass marbles and always wondered how the marbles could have possibly got there in the first place.

John also smoked; he had been taught properly by his benefactor. He was given a cigarette holder – the art of smoking for enjoyment and not irritating others was explained to him. Never ever should he smoke inside the house; the smoke was bad for children's lungs. He should only smoke after a day's work and a meal and, like eating, always stop just when you felt you wanted more. For these reasons during warm summer evenings John could be seen sitting on the Cotswold wall outside enjoying his cigarette.

If there was any art in him at all it manifested itself in one way only, namely the making of walking sticks. He walked for miles, those large boots swinging on the ends of those long legs as Gulliver walked through Lilliput. He would often walk through the woods and when spotting a straight ash or wild cherry he would peg it down so that next year he would have a ready made walking stick. He made use of the knotty pieces – some he had lopped for two or three consecutive years until the top was an ornament. If he found a ram's horn, it could not be wasted so he sat on the wall carving his shapes with a penknife. His sticks were naturally extra long and they were finished with a ferrule made by the local blacksmith. He was rightfully very proud of them and would take painstaking trouble to explain in detail the origin of each one.

Home rule from Ma

It was time to think about the evening meal. Ma was not very pleased with the prospect – those bones had had all the goodness boiled out of them. There was some swede left and a muslin bag filled with potatoes was suspended from the saucepan lid. She did have some stale bread however, so she put a whole loaf to soak in water. There were a few raisins still in the biscuit tin left from Christmas. She took them out and methodically removed the stones. After squeezing the surplus water from the bread she added two cups of brown sugar, the raisins and one egg she had left in the isinglass. Putting this mixture in her large baking tin, she placed knobs of dripping over the top – taking care not to let any of the gravy at the bottom go into the pudding. There was never much gravy left if her family had been given the chance to spread their own bread.

Ma sat making a pair of gloves while the pudding was cooking. She had actually earned fourpence. Queenie had gone to the park with her truck hoping to meet the others from school. They could see the dead and fallen pieces of wood much better than she could, so between them they would fill the truck and she would drag it home. Dora was again sent up to the shop for a ha'pennyworth of blackjack. Maybe it would help ease Jackie's cough.

It was time for the men to come home. Tom was first. He was nearly in tears. It was his scissors that had blistered his hands. They were sore and cracked and nearly the colour of leather. Ma, however, had no sympathy. 'Just pop outside and wash them, use plenty of carbolic soap, then rub them with snowfire, like your Dad.'

Joe came in carrying a letter in one hand and a bucket in the other in the other.

'What have you got in there Joe?' said Ma.

'Sit down and I'll tell you all,' he answered. 'They had a party at the palace last night – they had pheasants to eat; would you believe it, they only ate the breasts? They left all the rest in the dishes. The legs, wings, bones and even bits of stuffing. Cook made a stew for us today and even when the staff had all eaten this was left over.'

'What a windfall!'

The whole family were licking their lips and peering into the bucket.

Queenie had different ideas. 'That's real wicked. Folks who waste food like that will never go to heaven. Whether you're rich or poor, waste not, want not, that's what I say. One day they will regret their wickedness.'

'Their wickedness is our salvation. We will live like lords tonight,' retorted Ma. So saying she put the contents of the bucket into a saucepan with her apology for a stew.

'I don't mind them being wicked,' affirmed Dad. 'Their yesterday's wickedness will be our today's salvation. Get the big pot on, Ma.' So, toast forgotten, Ma busied herself with the pot and fire and Joe sat down immediately to read his expected letter from Victoria on Vancouver Island.

'All pull up your chairs,' said Ma, but Dad quietened down everyone's excitement, ready for grace. When order was achieved they all sang, 'Be Present at Our Table Lord'.

'I wonder if they sang grace at the Palace yesterday?' queried Queenie.

'Course not,' retorted Dad. 'How could they? They weren't as hungry as us when they pulled up their chairs. That's why they threw half of it away.'

Mum took Jackies's meal up to him on his usual enamel plate with the alphabet around the border. 'He would soon get better if he could always eat like this, Joe.'

There was audible chewing at the table. They ate, as only 'Oliver' knew how. Comments of appreciation and gratefulness were coming from all. Mother's mind went back to the gypsy – she was convinced.

They all confessed it was the best meal they had had since the Jubilee.

Joe was reading out loud the letter that the postman had given him. It had come from cousin Alf who had emigrated to Vancouver. He implored Joe to go. Joe kept very quiet while the bread pudding was placed in the centre of the table. It was placed on the same piece of newspaper that had been used all day. The pudding was cut into various sizes, and everyone helped himself or herself according to age. Each knew which was his or her piece – whether you were hungry or not was never questioned – tonight apart, they were always hungry. They held their pudding in their hands and enjoyed it. If ever plates were needed for pudding, Ma washed up the plates from the first course. Mostly however they made do. No one objected to apple pudding being served on a soupy plate. There was never anything of the first course left on the plate. It was getting the apple pudding that mattered. A very satisfied family sang lustily that night, 'We thank thee Lord.'

Queenie meant and believed the grace; Mother attributed their good fortune to the gypsy; but Joe was certain that it was his enterprise alone, knowing exactly the time the pig swill would be put out and which bucket was for him.

They all sat opened mouth while the letter was being read but at the word photograph they crowded nearer.

'Funny looking log cabin,' commented Dad.

'Very comfortable,' retorted Joe.

'Looks like rag hung up at the windows for curtains,' sneered Tom.

'It looks very clean,' said Joe. He clearly did not like their attitude. Dora however had spotted the most laughable part of their new mode of living. 'Look,' she said 'Their washing line! One of them has had to wash their socks and shirts.' The thought of how a man would ever know how to tackle the job just gave her the giggles. But the ever-observant Betty added to the frivolity by noticing that even on the line, the shirt sleeves were still rolled up.

Joe, not to be outdone, just commented that if they were not unrolled they would not need ironing. He prevented any more sneering comments by finishing the letter.

Mother cut the conversation dead the moment the letter was finished. 'We'll discuss that later Joe,' But Joe was determined. 'There's nothing to discuss Ma. I'm going.'

'When I'm in Canada, Mum, the first thing you'll get is money to pay the doctor's bill, then and only then will Jackie start to improve.'

Mother lit a candle for Queenie who was entrusted to take all the younger ones to 'the dyke' at the bottom of the garden. Rats often crossed the path and if the family kept together they were less likely to develop a fear of them. Why she was given a lighted candle she did not understand, although she protected it with her hands. It was seldom alight when they returned. This ritual was always adhered to together. It made double sure that everyone attended to the necessities of nature and there were no accidents during the night. Ma always boasted that her family were all dry at night by the time they were eighteen months old, and indeed they were.

Ma had ten babies (eleven including the one she lost last year) and never had there been any smell of urine in her house. 'I don't mind the smell of clean dirt but urine is abhorrent.'

On returning from the dyke they went to the wash house. The weather being very cold, they were allowed (as a special treat tonight) just a drop of hot water from the kettle. They used the same enamel bowl that was used for the dishes. They all washed together using the same water and the same 'flannel'. This was actually a small square of somebody's threadbare sheet. They dried their faces on a rough, hard towel that started life as a sack for seed corn. It was much too good to use on the floor so it had been converted into two towels; the whole family used them on alternate weeks.

In the wash house they had a long stool designed for the killing of pigs – indeed it was often lent out to neighbours for that purpose. When hands and face were dry, they sat on this stool and pushed down their socks, while Ma scrubbed each mudsplattered knee with carbolic soap. Ma had 'a thing about knees' which a neighbour's child who had recently died of lockjaw had prompted. This ritual was always strictly adhered to; there were many screams, some more genuine than others, but when she saw them dabbing rather than scrubbing their knees with that rough towel, she knew that her job had been correctly administered. The water had now finished its service so Ma picked up the bowl, went to the door and flung its contents as far as she could across the garden. They had no drain, they did not consider it a hardship. The bowl now had a telltale line encircling it, but it would do for the men later. The men never used warm water; they always went to the rain water butt under the spouting – even tonight when they must break the ice first.

The children were now given one candle between them and sent to bed. They slept on iron bedsteads with shiny brass knobs. Their beds were really straw palliasses but they did have sheets that had been rescued from the ragbag by girls in service. Blankets were non-existent in their room but there were several old coats and anyway you were allowed to keep on any clothes you needed. Sid always kept his socks on – he put them on after his Saturday night bath and he didn't see his toes again till the next Saturday.

The bedroom was small. It contained two double bedsteads and there was about a foot of space dividing them. There really was no space for undressing. Each chose their preferred place to sleep – last up the stairs

Mr Banbury, supervisor of The Olivet (the United Free Methodist Church), with his women helpers.

had no choice at all. The number in each bed often varied. Dad insisted that they went straight to sleep: if not they paid the price. His hand was strong – they knew Ma had a stick and often threatened, but she never used it and they knew she wouldn't. One of them usually managed to knock over the candle – so they often crept into bed in the dark.

The room was never cold in the winter or even hot in the summer, the walls were too thick for that. The window – permanently closed – was very small. The door however was always open to ensure that any disturbance could be heard. Their lungs had been filled with fresh country air all day and their limbs were physically tired so sleep was not a problem. Downstairs Ma had taken a blue-red brick from the oven. She wrapped it in a yellowish scorched-coloured square of sheet and took it up stairs to her bed. She never pampered herself but she had determined tonight that the warmth from her body might ease Jackie's coughing.

When her chores were finished, Tom and Joe had washed, Queenie was sewing and Dad was repairing those nosebags, it was now time for a family discussion. Decisions were always made at this hour, after all children were in bed. Tonight she was terrified. She knew that Joe had had a letter – he was her favourite offspring, if indeed there was a favourite. She knew he was hardworking and genuine – he always made his own decisions and indeed he was usually proved right. He could never be accused of 'drifting along with the tide'. So it was that, as Ma descended the stairs Joe started his well-rehearsed speech.

'It's no use, Ma, my mind is made up. I'm twenty-one and can do as I like. If my allotment does well this year I shall enter every show I can. I've saved all my prize money from last year so I shall have enough to pay my fare. I shall borrow from Uncle Jack for my "landing money" then I'll send it straight back to him.'

Ma covered her face with both hands. 'Joe, we shall never see you again. Six thousand miles is a long way from home. George and Charlie are still in the fens…'

'Don't fret so,' Joe interrupted. 'George and Charlie are coming home this summer – they'll be home before I go – you won't have a bed spare to sleep me anyway. I'm working from half past six in the morning till five at night – six days a week. What do I get? Eight shillings and sixpence. I'll be poor all my life if I stay here. I could never ask a girl to marry me. It wouldn't be fair.'

Dad slapped him on the shoulder. 'Whatever you do, Joe, I'm sure it will be for the best. We shall manage. That clock has nearly got to nine now – the paraffin has nearly gone.' Very abruptly he put his mouth over the chimney of the lamp and blew it out. 'You can't burn a candle at both ends.' Together they felt their way up the stone stairs and in the darkness Joe was consoling his mother, but Ma had decided to concentrate on the gypsy's prediction. Perhaps it would never happen.

Sid's escapades

The children went to the local church school. On a few Christian special days, the pupils would attend church in the morning, then be given the day off. It was Ash Wednesday and Sid knew it would happen. He hated it, he hated parading to church – he thought going to church should be kept for Sundays. Dad had asked him to take old Blossom, the mare, down to the river where Ben was hurdle making.

'Come up to the farm as soon as you leave church,' Dad said temptingly. What a thought! Had he got to sit through the service and dream about it! He could not resist the temptation. As the long row of pupils was nearing the church, Sid slipped the ranks and bolted to the farm. Hearing his name being called only had the effect of making him run faster. He knew he would pay the penalty tomorrow, but it was worth it.

At the farm he found Blossom already tethered to a post. She was thirty years old now but very dependable. Dad was surprised to see him so soon, but he had already harnessed the mare with collar and hames. The traces were hanging on the hames so Sid quickly glanced around for a sack. He threw it over her back, then led her to the staddle stone to enable him to mount. What a glorious day to be out on your own, walking a horse. The river was about two miles away but church was almost forgotten. Ben was lopping willow trees today and Blossom was needed to prevent any branches falling into the river. It was a simple task for Blossom but it was the sense of responsibility that Sid relished.

The day went well. Sid enjoyed every minute of it. When the lopping was finished Ben allowed Sid to saw some lengths of willow. He showed him how to bark the wood and how to rend the lengths. Sid admired Ben's skill – what beautiful well-made hurdles.

It was a very happy Sid who wended his way homeward on the bare back of Blossom. He was whistling all the way, never even sparing one thought for the punishment tomorrow. 'It'll come,' said Sid. 'Why worry about it?'

During the summer months, when the roads were dry and dusty, the children could often be seen filtering the dust through their fingers. They wrote messages in the sand and played chasing games. It was, however, much easier for carthorses to negotiate the roads in the summer and the council made sure that loads of large granite stones were hauled from quarry to roadside and left in piles where the deepest mud appeared in the winter. A few old men were employed to break these stones and place them in the deepest ruts. A job obviously for people with more brawn than brain. These large stones would frequently break where least expected. Small sharp flint-like chips would fly off in any direction. For this reason Sid was always told to keep right away – 'Very dangerous,' said Dad, and Dad expected him to do as he was told.

It was on such a day towards the end of February that thoughtless Sid was tempted to stand and stare. The old man offered him his hammer suggesting that he had a go. It took all his strength to lift the tool but the force of gravity alone ensured that it came down with great weight. A needle-like splinter fled on impact straight to Sid's eye. He crumpled up on the ground. His screams could be heard down the length of the road and there was soon a mob of well wishers and nosey parkers. One gave him a glass of whisky; one of the local runners ran to the palace for ice, thinking a cold compress would ease the pain. Queenie openly prayed – Father cursed the boy for being disobedient but when Joe arrived from work, he counted his pennies and found just enough for the train fare to Oxford. So, carrying Sid over his shoulder like a sack of potatoes he made off to the railway station en route to Oxford Eye Hospital.

Joe was already tired after a long day's work, and the shock of finding Sid in this state and carrying him to the station had drained him physically. It was quite a long walk from Oxford station to the Eye Hospital but he fought on manfully. Repentant Sid was appreciating the strength of his eldest brother. After the offending splinter had been removed a bandage was applied and instructions were given to Joe that it was not to be removed for a se'night. It was impossible to tell the extent of permanent damage. It was also impossible to return home that night so they sat huddled together on a seat in the railway waiting room.

Sid slept but not Joe, his body ached, he was hot and restless. He had never felt like this before. What happened Joe never knew – but when he regained consciousness he was in a ward of the Woodstock workhouse. He had lain between life and death for a fortnight. The matron explained how indebted he was to the Duchess. She had sent him food daily, blankets for his bed; she had in fact pulled him through a bout of pneumonia. A subdued Sid came to visit him, proudly showing the scar on his eye. The scar would remain for the rest of his life – but his sight had miraculously not suffered. Everyone was well again and Ma once more leaned on the gypsy.

A generous visit from the Duchess – but the truth is told

It was on a Tuesday early in March that Ma was wakened at half past five. Outside the window, sheep were bleating, men and boys were shouting and sticks were banging on the walls. Dad did not stir, he had arrived home the previous that evening very tired indeed. On the farm the season's threshing had just been completed. Dad usually cut the bonds or fed the box but this year he had been obliged to take charge of the corn. Each sack weighed two hundredweight and that was the limit of his strength. The gaffer came round very frequently to scrutinise the sample. It wasn't good, Dad knew that; the weather was too dry last summer. If the sample was good the mood of the boss would make the hours pass more quickly. This year was the opposite. There was far more dust than usual and when Dad arrived home he was compared to a chimney sweep.

'That sample won't pass for malting. It will have to be used for barley meal,' grunted the boss. 'I'll see what offers I can get in the market tomorrow.'

On this particular market day Mum knew there would be plenty of sheep. She roused her husband, then continued her usual morning chores. 'I could hear plenty of drover lads this morning.' She put it to him partly as a statement and partly as a question. 'Yes,' he confirmed 'There's a lot of barren ewes coming in from Tackley today. The butchers will get a lot of tough mutton this week.'

'Tough or no,' said Ma, 'I'd like to get my hands on some of it.'

'Each one of those ewes has been kept a year for nothing. I told him he needed a young ram but he wouldn't listen,' said knowledgeable Dad. But Dad was right as he usually was and when the farmer said he couldn't afford a new ram, Dad suggested he should sell two ewes. That way his flock would now be profitable.

Coughing was continuing ceaselessly; Jackie showed no sign of improving. 'I think we should have the doctor in,' Ma confided in Queenie. Dad's mind however was on his day's work. 'I might manage to catch a few rooks today; there's a lot around this year. I'm broadcasting barley in the top field, and I'm being allowed to use the new harrows.'

As Joe came down the coughing was obviously worse. Joe's mind was made up. 'I think we should give up every penny to pay for the doctor. Shall I call as I go to work, Ma?'

Ma knew that the ultimate decision was hers and she gave Joe the nod. If only her brother John was here he would have offered to help.

Joe sniffed. 'Smells like a good breakfast today – is that an egg?'

'Yes,' said Ma. 'Your Dad picked up the first three plover eggs – one for Dad, one for you and one for Jackie. That will do him good.'

So, as Joe went to the palace that morning, he called at the doctor's and asked him to visit. Ma already felt easier because she knew Jackie was going to get attention.

Today was also the last day of Betty's home life. Most of her uniform had been made or scrounged. Her situation had been found. Today she would buy her rail ticket and tomorrow she would face the outside world alone. Ma only had four children to send to school now – in theory she should be very well off. When, years ago, she produced four sons consecutively, she was the envy of all. Sons brought money into a family and made it rich, but in practice it wasn't working out for her. Queenie wished she could go into service, but Ma always explained that if she were meant for service, she would have been given perfect eyesight.

Betty started the day by packing her few essentials into a box and Ma gave her exactly sixpence to purchase her rail ticket, 'That is the last money you will get from me. From now on you must fend for yourself. You must be sure to save two or three pennies each week. Then you will be able to buy a new hat or boots.'

'From now on I will buy nothing in Woodstock, I shall shop in Oxford. The first purchase will be a pair of shoes, I can't wear boots any longer.' Betty really was desperate to kick the traces.

It was barely eleven o' clock when Ma could hear a horse's hooves and, straining to peer through the curtains, she caught a glimpse of a pony and trap nearing the cottage. She recognised it immediately as the one owned by the Duchess of Marlborough.

'Pop upstairs, Queenie, she won't want to see you,' said Ma as she was turning over her dirty apron and adjusting her hair combs. Ma curtseyed as she opened the door saying, 'Good morning, your grace.'

'I have heard from Joe that your little Jackie is very poorly. I wondered if you have everything you need for him.' She spoke as a fairy godmother and indeed she was looked upon as that in the neighbourhood.

Ma assured her that she could manage and each phrase was punctuated by 'Your grace'.

'I have called on the doctor and asked him to send the bill to me, so you'll not have to worry about that bill,' she said in sympathetic tones.

'Thank you, Your Grace, thank you, Your Grace,' she reiterated because she could think of nothing else to say.

'Do you have a hot water bottle?' she questioned.

'We have a brick for him, thank you Your Grace,' she answered.

'I have brought you a real bottle,' said the Duchess producing a stone-water bottle with a screw top. 'And here is a bottle of Bovril as well. I will also ask cook to prepare him a meal every day if Joe will remember to collect it.'

'Thank you, Your Grace, thank you, Your Grace,' she said bobbing up and down.

'God bless you all,' said the Duchess as she disappeared through the doorway.

Queenie opened the opposite door as the front one closed. 'I heard all that,' she admitted. 'I was only sitting on the stairs.'

'Isn't she kind, Queenie?'

But Queenie was not convinced. She walked across the room and, putting her hand on the family bible, she quoted: 'It is easier for a camel to go through the eye of a needle than for a rich man to enter the kingdom of Heaven. Mark 10:25.'

'Hush Queenie,' Ma restrained her. 'You are so critical of the rich, you must learn to accept your station. Blessed are the meek for they shall inherit the earth. Matthew 5:5.'

Then, after peering through the window again, 'Here comes the doctor.' This time Queenie could not be hustled out, as the doctor would use the stairs. He admitted himself into the room following a powerful bang on the door. He had a very deep voice and abrupt manner, showing no sympathy.

'So you have decided to send for me at last. I've heard your youngest has been coughing for months,' he was scolding her.

Ma's usual dominant character left her. She felt small, inefficient and guilty, as if she must now wait for the punishment.

'I didn't have the money before,' she trembled.

'You have not got it now,' he contradicted her, succeeding in keeping her in a state of nervous tension.

In two strides he was across the room and up the stairs followed meekly by mother. Queenie sat still, straining her keen ears in vain.

They descended the stairs much more slowly and deliberately. Then, after closing the door, Ma uttered just two words: 'Well, doctor?'

With very slow but certain movements he shook his head again and again. After a deathly silence she tried two more words, 'You mean...'

His answer was equally slow and equally deliberate, but this time his head was nodding and the truth had sunk deep into Ma. Queenie knew too; although she had not witnessed the shake or nod, there was something about the silence that spelt it out clearly to her.

The doctor put his hand on the latch of the door and half opened it, then turning back, he said in apologetic tones, 'I'm sorry. Even if you had called me earlier, there is nothing I could have done. May God bless you all.' He was gone. Ma collapsed into her wicker chair covering her face with her two large capable hands.

'That will be the second we have taken to the churchyard. Poor little Jackie! Do we have to see him suffer so?'

Queenie knew that Ma needed strength now. She must never be seen crying in front of the children, so Queenie quietly called on her Maker to find the right words for her.

'If trouble is sent from God, he will also give us the strength to overcome it. There is no suffering in heaven. Let us keep praying – miracles still happen sometimes. Let's get busy now and take no thought for the morrow. We will have the rest of the family in soon.'

It was just at that moment that Betty returned with her rail ticket.

'Why the tears?' she said, feeling the gloom in the household.

'The news is bad about Jackie. The doctor can't do nothing,' said Queenie sharply, so that Mother was not forced into speaking. She need not have worried. By now Ma's steely character was coming back. She had decided to keep control. She now felt re-armed.

'Don't say any more, either of you. Just get on with your jobs. It's not to be mentioned again till the young ones are in bed.' She spoke so emphatically that Queenie knew that Ma was in control of the situation. She admired Ma for her courage and endurance under stress. In Queenie's language it would have been 'guts'.

The three boisterous children were soon heard approaching and as the door was flung open they chorused, 'We've got tuppence, we've got tuppence.'

Such a complete change of atmosphere was welcomed by all and the children were quick to explain their good luck.

'We helped drive some sheep to the slaughter house. The butcher gave it to us.' That butcher would never know how that tuppence had helped this family today. The children did not guess that anything was amiss.

Ma spent the afternoon ironing and hanging the garments on the line above her. At times she was very quiet. She wanted to keep away from Jackie; she felt she had let him down badly – she knew something now that he did not. She forced herself upstairs to face him, she wanted to pick up that frail little body and squeeze it. She wanted to say, 'I'm sorry, I'm sorry, I'm sorry.' She could not trust herself to be alone with him. Queenie's words kept haunting her:

'If trouble is sent from God, He will give you strength to overcome.'

Tom was first to arrive home from work, as he threw open the door he made a statement that clearly expected an explanation. 'You've had the Duchess today!'

'How do you know?' asked Queenie.

'Oh! They always discuss other people's business in the factory. That bit of news did not escape their notice. They were all speculating on why she came.'

'She has been very kind,' said Ma, making doubly sure that Queenie couldn't air her views of the Duchess. 'She brought some things for Jackie. A real hot water bottle.'

'That's very kind of her. A little help is worth a lot of sympathy. Here's a letter, Ma – the postman just gave it to me.' It was clear from the chatter that the dark cloud hanging over the family had gone unnoticed.

Ma looked at the letter, scrutinising the postmark and the handwriting. She put it in her apron pocket, deciding that too could wait until the children were in bed.

Joe was next to arrive home. He too was full of excitement about his day's work. He had walked from the monument plain to the palace for

Jackie's meal; 'We've planted thousands of trees now across the plain, all in battle formation. They'll last for hundreds of years. Very clever man who drew up the plans we use. I love measuring and planting – just like going back in history,' Joe said excitedly.

'Do you love it enough to stay here?' enquired Ma.

'No, Ma – I shall definitely go when the last flower show is over and I've counted my money,' said Joe emphatically.

'Go straight out to wash Joe, while the bowl is not being used. Your Dad will need it the moment he comes in,' prompted Ma.

But just at that moment Dad did come in. He lifted the latch in the same excited state. He was carrying a lump of fat bacon. 'Gaffer gave it to me. You see he did very well in market today. It seems that samples of barley are poor everywhere this year so his sold for malting. I shall be going to the Adam and Eve tonight. He is giving free drinks all round.' Then raising his voice in a taunting manner he shouted, 'Are you coming, Joe? Free beer!'

Joe's head immediately appeared through the wash house doorway.

'You know my answer Dad, I'm going down to the Olivet. There's a missionary coming tonight with a magic lantern. Would you like to come, Queenie? You'll enjoy it even if you can't see the pictures. We shall sing lots of hymns.'

Ma announced that if all the family were going out, she herself would sit upstairs with Jackie until the paraffin failed. She would make another glove.

Today The Olivet is a private house.

Oxford Street looking north. The Adam and Eve has a dark overhanging sign towards the end, on the right.

'I'll go and see him now,' said Joe. 'I'll tell him about the new lambs in the park.'

The meal was very noisy that night. Each had his or her special topic, each felt that 'everything in the world is good'. The three females alone were keeping up the masquerade.

Betty's uppermost thoughts throughout the day were naturally on her career. She was, after all, on the threshold of life. To her, tomorrow would be her most important day. Ma would have been pestering her with do's and don'ts but Betty had been relieved of this by the gloom that overshadowed her mother's thoughts. After the meal, Ma looked under her cushion and took out another precious newspaper. She cut it very carefully into perfect squares, then pushed Dad's sacking needle and string through the corner of the squares, securing them together.

Queenie was handed the paper and sent on her nightly errand to the privy. Dad was complaining about toothache. He got no sympathy from anyone tonight, least of all Ma. He usually proffered some excuse when he intended to go to the pub. Nothing would prevent Dad from receiving his free beer tonight.

The evening rituals were completed but there was no mention of the family situation until the door had closed behind the retiring children. Only then Ma sat down and took out the dreaded letter from her pocket.

'Who is it from?' said Dad.

'It's from Charlie,' answered Ma. 'I know his writing. Something is wrong – George always writes the letters.' Silence reigned while Ma opened and read the letter (with help from Joe).

It explained that, as George had a persistent cough, they would soon be coming home again.

'It will be good to get them home,' admitted Dad.

'I'm glad I didn't go,' confessed Joe. 'I don't like the sound of it.'

'Now,' said Ma in a very slow, shaky voice as if choosing each word individually. 'I – have – one – more – shock – for – you. The doctor came today.'

'What did he say?' 'What did he do?' 'Did he give him a tonic?' Questions came thick and fast, all expecting a quick, sudden cure.

'He – said – nothing.'

'Nothing,' echoed the chorus.

'He just shook his head,' said Ma, shaking her head slowly to reinforce the message; but the message had gone home. Dad could not speak, Tom could not speak. Joe, as always, was the only one who knew what to do.

'Let us go on our knees,' he said and all obeyed him. 'The family will unite in prayer.' Dad didn't really believe in this but he could not ridicule Joe in this time of shock.

'Oh Lord, come into this house. Look upon its youngest member and, if it be Thy will, may he not be taken from us. Thy will be done. Amen.' Automatically they repeated, 'Amen!'

After an uneasy silence when all were too shocked and dazed to speak, it was Ma who broke in.

'Now, what do you all think of doing this evening?'

Dad clearly was not going to be diverted.

'If I stay at home, I shall neither cure Jackie nor bring home the boys. If I go out, I might cure my toothache.'

In quiet subdued tones, after deep consideration, Joe determined: 'I shall still go to the Olivet, I've promised to take my melodium for the hymns. Are you coming Queenie?'

'Yes, I love singing,' was the abrupt answer.

Betty was advised to go to bed early, tomorrow was so important and,

The Adam and Eve as it is today, a private house.

from now on, she would be getting up much earlier.

Tom was plucking up courage, when at last he ventured, 'Dad, can I come with you?'

'I should think not,' answered Ma so quickly that Dad didn't even get a chance to give his views. 'You can go with Joe.'

'No, thank you,' he said emphatically. 'I've finished with that. I'll go out for a run. I intend to be town runner next time around so I must put in some practice.'

'Good idea,' snapped Joe, 'I'm packing it in anyway, but you'll have to work hard – your job does not help you. Get stuck into it everyday.'

'Oh dear! Where will he find the money for new boots?' Ma's worries were piling up. Her legs were heavy as she dragged them up the stairs. She had a lighted paraffin lamp in one hand, while a rolled up bundle in the other contained one unstitched glove. She would be asleep when they all came home, the oil would not last long. Never once during this fateful day did she think about the gypsy, so she was neither credited nor blamed for the events.

A white funeral

It was the middle of March, early on a Tuesday morning, when Jackie's short life ebbed away. All the curtains in the house were drawn together and left in that position till after the funeral.

Mother crept into the bedroom of the three youngest ones and told them that Jackie had gone to see Jesus.

The quiet, thoughtful Sarah acted so unexpectedly: she dissolved into tears and sobbed bitterly. Sid put on a grown-up air and said, 'You've got me, Ma, I'll help you all I can.' This was so unlike Sid, feeling so sorry for his mother. Dora said, 'I'll be the youngest now Ma, I'm glad Jackie won't be able to cough any more.'

It was Ma who washed him and laid him straight in his best white Sunday shirt. She allowed the younger ones to see him. Indeed she encouraged it. 'I don't hold with being afraid of death,' she said.

The doctor suggested that he be taken to the mortuary in the workhouse because they had no suitable place to keep him. Mother was furious – 'No way will he leave this house until he is carried to the churchyard.' The doctor said no more. He knew that if Ma had a breakdown now, she might be taken to the lunatic asylum and the children could well find their way to the workhouse. This was a time for the family to unite. Joe called on the Rector to ask for the bell to toll but everyone else went about his or her work. Dad, Joe and Tom all got to work on time and likewise the children to school.

Ma walked around the house with smouldering lavender . She often did this: it was her remedy for any smells.

She then went to the undertaker and chose the white box. Long before anyone came home, the white clad infant was lying in it, in the wash house. No one thought this peculiar, the doctor insisted that he must not be either in a bedroom or in the living room.

The days before the funeral were busy. Frequent visits to see him were encouraged. Many school friends were brought in. They played with him in life so it was natural to visit him in death. The funeral was arranged for Saturday afternoon, which would be least disruptive for all. Betty was notified and she arranged to swap her half day from Wednesday to Saturday. Each black tie, hat, gloves etc. that had been packed away after the last 'event' saw the light of day again. Any article that could not be found would be borrowed. Dad had a black suit and a real black bowler (kept in a box under the bed). He often helped others at these events, because the payment was usually of the type of which he approved.

They had a dress rehearsal on Friday to ensure there were enough clothes for all – some were too small, some too large, but they must be able to walk in them.

The time was drawing near. Every house in the street had its curtains drawn as a mark of respect. So the small white coffin carried by the four youngest members of the family headed the cortège that crawled slowly towards the church. The tenor bell sounded a heavy boom every few seconds. In the church they sang 'There's a Friend for Little Children'. There were so many children in church the rector suggested they sang alone. Their very small voices in the very large church sang 'Jesus Meek and Gentle'. The bell was still tolling. Following the rector, the procession in similar style headed back to the cemetery. There, at the end of a long row of small graves, Jackie was placed. All locals were either there or represented. They didn't exactly enjoy funerals but it relieved the monotony of their humdrum life. It gave them a different topic for conversation and comments were varied.

'So and so's hat.' 'Somebody's veil.' 'Did you hear that cough?' 'He'll be the next.' The cause of death was just whispered. 'Consumption', no child must ever hear that.

On returning home, the curtains were pulled back immediately. The black garbs were discarded until Sunday and the children ran out to play. Balls were rebounding against the house so the girls appeared happy and Sid was bowling his noisy steel hoop down the road. They had a feeling of great satisfaction – this was the second time in a year they had been called upon; they had come through with flying colours, indeed they were the envy of their school friends.

On Sunday morning the entire family 'dressed up' again and went to morning service. This was the memorial service and the rector spoke personally to them. As Joe and Queenie were members of The United Methodist Church, the family were invited there for the evening service. Whether each one attended or not was never questioned but you did nothing to jeopardise either Jackie's or indeed your own entry 'to that place in the bright blue sky.'

Mother enjoyed the chapel service. She knew they would sing 'Safe in the Arms of Jesus', they always did. She knew also that this was the one hymn to which her strong character succumbed. When the hymn started, so did the tears, slowly at first, but gathering speed they silently found their way unhindered to the floor. She did not sniff or sob, neither did she take out a handkerchief. She knew that she would leave the chapel with a newfound strength to meet the harsh unpredictable realities that awaited her.

As she packed away those clothes on that Monday morning Ma's thoughts turned toward the next time they would be needed. They had been used much too frequently in recent years. George and Charlie were not notified, firstly because they did not always work in the same place, and secondly Ma did not think it warranted bringing them home.

The memory of the gypsy for the moment had deserted her.

Farm life in the raw

It was nearly the end of March and Ma thought that, as the days were getting longer and warmer, it was time to get the spring routines in hand. Twice annually, at the burst and fall of leaf, she gave the members of her family a 'dose of physic'. This was intended to prevent any sluggishness in the digestive system. She used senna pods – she steeped them overnight and put them into the breakfast teapot. This way their presence was never even suspected and no one escaped. Treatment so early in the day ensured that no rest was interrupted. She liked to get the internal 'spring clean' finished first, before she started on the house and finally the more personal items of clothing such as coats and trousers.

The farm where Dad worked was mostly arable. They kept one sow to ensure plenty of pig meat and one cow plus her last two heifer calves. Most of the year there was milk and maybe butter. Bluebell was the spoilt friend of all on the farm. She usually calved in spring, that being nature's way to ensure plenty of grass for her keep. The boss would have liked more cows but the initial cost was too much. His only hope was that Bluebell would supply another heifer calf. Last year it was one bull calf but the year before that it was twin heifers, and now they were nearly old enough to visit the bull.

Bluebell had been dry for some time and her calf was expected soon. Ma was looking forward with mixed feelings. There would be benefits like milk and cherry curd but there were disadvantages: if a heifer calf arrived the boss would celebrate with his men. She put that thought at the back of her mind; it might never happen.

So, at about two o'clock in the morning on this particular day, a handful of small stones were tossed up at their bedroom window to awaken Dad. Ma woke first and went to the window to investigate. She returned to rouse Dad. 'Bluebell needs help,' she said. Out of bed he sprang, collecting his trousers from the brass knob of the bedstead. He jumped into them, slipping the braces over his shoulders and making his way downstairs as he did so. If Bluebell needed help he would be there. Ma lay down again, but sleep

Barn Piece Farm, where George worked, has been a private house since 1962.

eluded her. So, bored by lying awake and worried about Dad's return, she was downstairs by four o'clock that morning. She lit the fire and made the tea. She drank the first cup on her own, standing the teapot on the hob to keep warm. What to do at this early hour she did not know, it would be unprofitable to light a lamp in order to make a glove, so to help ease her mind and overcome her boredom she drank another cup of tea, yes and another. She had completely forgotten that the teapot had been put ready with the senna.

She felt rather guilty and indulgent. She had never drunk so much tea before and still Dad had not returned. Queenie came down, so, to prevent Queenie's questions, Ma picked up the teapot and threw the rest on the garden, to prepare a fresh pot. Then and only then did she notice the remains of the senna pods. What had she done? Even then she thought first of the wasted senna pods. The effect of such a strong dose on her digestive system she could totally cover up, she was sure. I'll jump that hurdle if or when I meet it, she told herself.

'Would you wake up Joe now, Queenie? I know it's early but I want him to run to the farm to see how things are progressing.'

'I'll go myself,' said Queenie.

'Indeed, you will not,' answered Ma. 'That's no place for a girl.'

'Why not?' she retorted.

'Because I said so, now don't ask any more questions. Just wake up Joe,' ordered Ma.

Queenie knew that Ma always had to be obeyed, if not always understood.

When she returned Ma was singing 'Safe in the Arms of Jesus'. Queenie knew it was being sung to divert her thoughts from the present topic.

Joe came down promising to go and be back quickly, but he reminded his mother that it was Tom who wanted to be a runner soon.

Tom was awake. The two lads slept so close together, so, very un-Tom like, he came down early.

'What is all the commotion today?' he enquired.

'It's Bluebell who's calving. She is such a good milker that a heifer calf would be very valuable,' explained Ma.

'What rubbish! I don't believe it,' said Tom. 'If Bluebell gives lots of milk, it doesn't mean that her calf would.'

'Well, I don't know about these things,' conceded Ma. 'Joe's a long time, I wonder what has happened to his running.'

Tom turned aside and whispered in undertones to Queenie, 'I expect he has called at his allotment to measure how much his onions have grown during the night. I will show him how to run. What Joe can do, I can do.'

'Like Bluebell and her calf,' taunted Ma.

'Oh, that's different,' Tom kept up his argument.

'Tom,' asked Ma, 'When you are in the park collecting acorns to plant, which tree do you get them from?'

'The King Tree by High Lodge, of course,' he responded.

'Why do you choose that one?' she continued, trying to outwit him.

'Because acorns from the biggest tree are likely to grow into the biggest trees and live the longest,' Tom assured her.

'Isn't that exactly the same?' Ma was confident she had penetrated his stubbornness. 'You can't put an old 'ead on young shoulders, Tom.' She changed the subject: 'I can hear Joe coming.'

'You are not to keep him any breakfast,' said Joe. 'Bluebell is not making much progress, so they gave Dad some cider and bread with cold bacon. He won't be back for some time yet but he will be sure to come back before he starts his day's work.'

'I should think so,' commented Tom. 'How's your onions, Joe?'

'How did you know I went there?' he demanded.

'Cos you can't keep away,' Tom jested.

'Well, everything looks fine. I am already counting my prize money, if you must know. Those roses I planted are making good progress. I'll show 'em,' said cocky Joe.

Joe was very proud of his roses. He collected briars from the hedgerows. Dad would often locate one for him. He searched the copses and spinneys, then uprooted them and transplanted them to his allotment. When the head gardener at Blenheim was pruning his roses in early spring, Joe would rescue and label the prunings and graft the best buds onto his own wild roses. In this way he had the best, most up-to-date novelties on the market. They were admired and envied by all.

'Will you still be going to Canada, Joe?' asked Tom.

'I don't intend to allow anything to stand in my way. My bed will be needed anyway.' Everyone was still trying to dissuade him.

'I wish you two would get off to work – you'll be late,' said Ma.

The brothers went on their way while Queenie called down the other three.

'Eggs for breakfast,' called a delighted Sarah. 'What sort are they?'

'Never you mind,' said Ma. 'You eat them up, they'll do you good – and when you come home from school, I think you'll be getting some cherry curds.'

'Goody!' they all echoed.

Dad loved the peewits and many hundreds there were. They are so good for the farmland that he devised his own method for their survival. During March he walked each available field picking up each egg he could find. The fields were now ready for spring planting. As soon as April arrived he would be just as determined that each nest would survive. This way the family had plenty of eggs to eat in March but the plovers benefited as well – they multiplied. Thousands of peewits swooped and screamed overhead as the horses pulled each implement across the fields. Dad had pre-located every nest; he stopped the horse and carefully replaced the eggs in their nest site. Maybe he was using the drill, the harrows or a roller – the eggs were often handled several times. So apart from the screaming overhead, this suited all. Sometimes there were day old chicks to contend with – they were strong and could run fast. Much to the distraught parent, he would catch one and take it to show the children. Dad and the birds were mutual friends. Dad loved birds, except of course the birds of prey. Birds were, like their way of life, either good or bad. Like the keeper, you did everything possible to protect them, or everything possible to destroy them.

So this morning they had enjoyed a breakfast of plover's eggs and then been ushered off to school when, only a few yards from home, they met Dad returning from the farm.

Dad took hold of Sid by the scruff of the neck and brought him back to the house allowing the girls to go on to school.

Dad was carrying one of those multi-purpose white enamel bowls and the cork of a bottle was peeping from his pocket.

'We've won! You'll never guess.' Dad was bubbling over with excitement. 'Bluebell had twins and they are both heifers. There's a drink for all today. How's that?' So saying he pulled from his pocket a bottle of whisky, holding it high with excitement.

'I don't relish that, I'll not taste it,' said Ma emphatically. 'But let's see what's in that bowl, that's a different matter.'

After one glance into the bowl, she jumped up and down with delight. She was sure they were the best cherry curds she had ever seen. The existence of a whole bottle of whisky she wanted to forget. Whisky for Dad spelt trouble for Ma. It had happened before.

'Why have you brought Sid home?' she demanded. 'I know you won't approve, but this time I'm the boss,' said Dad, growing in confidence even before the bottle was opened.

'Sid is not going to school today. He is going up to the top field to keep the rooks and pigeons off the seeds.' Then, looking Sid straight in the eye: 'Go and get the bird scarer and, if you keep them off all day, you will have earned tuppence. How's that? Better than school? School is alright for them wenches, but not for growing lads, eh Sid?'

Sid virtually grew up in those few minutes. It did his ego a power of good, he swelled with pride and it clearly showed on his face. He mattered at last; he was of some use to someone.

'Thank you Dad,' he said with genuine gratitude.

'It'll seem like a long day Sid. You've got to show what metal you're made of today. You'll be tempted to sit down or even sleep,' warned Dad.

'Not me, never,' Sid assured him.

'Now, fetch the white coat, and let's see how it fits you.'

Mum was clearly against the scheme. She was worried about the ensuing visit from the school inspector. She was not prepared to lie about Sid's absence although Dad obviously was.

'If you do wrong, you must put up with the consequences,' she added, 'Now drink a cup of tea, and get back to work.'

Ma's 'tea' was beginning to take effect and she wanted to be left alone.

'I'm not eating or drinking at the moment,' he confessed. 'I am not going to work either. See this bottle?' He held it aloft again 'I'm going to drink the whole lot, except for the last mouthful – that's for Bill. He is going to pull out my bad teeth today. I shall never get another bottle of whisky, so that's settled. It works better on an empty belly. He is going to do it in the barn where no one can hear my screams.'

'Oh dear! Oh dear!' Ma wailed. 'You'll come home drunk. Drunk as a lord. What shall I do? What shall I do?'

Queenie consoled her mother. Even she approved of the use of whisky as medicine. She had heard too much about her Dad's toothache in recent weeks. She was 'right glad' that it would be gone forever.

Dad was sure he could stand it, he was sure Bill could do it. 'When I get to that glorious high pitch,' he boasted, 'out will come those teeth.'

'I hope you'll get past that glorious high pitch before you reach home.' Ma was nearly praying. 'Who would have thought that Bluebell could have caused all this uproar today!'

After he was out of hearing distance, Queenie suggested a prayer but Ma would have none of it.

'If a woman has toothache, Queenie, she just suffers in silence. If a man has toothache he uses it as the best reason ever suggested for drinking a whole bottle of whisky. It's me who needs the prayer, Queenie.' So saying she jumped up and ran to the bottom of the garden. By now she had a real 'pain under the pinny' and she could confide in no one. Queenie took out her patchwork and Ma herself took out her gloves, but she did not stitch. She thought of Sid, bashing the tin around the top field. Maybe Dad had devised that noise to cover any screams from the farm. She thought of the possibility of Dad's backing out at the last minute, but she dismissed that idea in the knowledge that his pub mates would duck him in the lake at any sound of cowardice.

Queenie answered another knock on the door to find the postman offering her a penny to deliver another telegram to Home Farm. She grabbed at the chance and was gone – Ma, too was gone… to the bottom of the garden again.

As she returned, she could distinctly hear Dad singing 'Onward Christian Soldiers'. She recognised his voice although there was a definite slur. It told her all; she would have preferred to run away, but she was his wife and years ago she had promised to obey, even if she was ill and he was dead drunk. She would be submissive, it was her duty. Bluebell had a lot to answer for. The consequences she would worry about tomorrow. As soon as she saw him she knew that the operation had been successful and as soon as he saw her he knew he would be successful too. She coolly ascended those stairs with her hand on that awful stomach – she was not afraid of him but she knew the meaning of 'love, honour and obey, in sickness and in health'. She wasn't quite sure whose sickness it was today, or whose health.

So when Queenie arrived home later Ma was staggering down the stairs, exhausted for a multitude of reasons. She carefully explained to Queenie that Dad was very tired because of his loss of sleep – yes, the offending teeth were gone – all he needed now was rest.

'So I suggested that he went to bed.' That was Ma's first 'white lie'. 'Let's have a cup of tea now, Queenie. I need one.'

Ma sat down and thought over the day's events. She now had a real worry; a worry she could not share. She was forty-four years old – maybe too old. Would the gypsy help?

Aspects of spring

In the washhouse of that small cottage stood two – and often three – large earthenware pans. Ma used these for making wine. Dad liked her wine even if it was second best to a pub visit. He didn't have to pay for it. In every odd corner of the cottage there stood a large earthenware jar. Ma thought that a jug of wine might often ease that craving he had to 'lift the latch'. He often bragged that he could 'lift the latch' even if he only had one penny.

There were other benefits from having plenty of homemade wine available. The butcher called occasionally – he enjoyed a jug of wine. The butcher usually killed his beasts on Tuesday and cut up the carcasses on Wednesday. Most of the best joints that would be sold at the weekend were put in the cellar. The offal and cheaper joints were sold in mid-week. The butcher had to be very skilled in allocating his meat both to satisfy his customers and yet make sure his cellar was empty on Saturday night. He knew every whim of every customer, who liked the fat joints and who liked the lean, who had a large enough pot to boil a cow's head, who liked free bones for making soup. No matter how shrewd the butcher was in cutting his joints, there were some Saturdays when he did not have sufficient to satisfy and some weeks when meat was left over. So as the butcher delivered at weekends, joints were sometimes larger or even smaller than ordered. This system being so primitive, Saturday evening customers had no choice and sometimes no meat. Sometimes the butcher would wrap up scraps and leftovers, and take it to the cottage. If Ma's family had not been to the butchers, he knew there was no money. A jug of wine made a fair swap.

Another admirer of Ma's wine was the local gamekeeper. His job did not allow him to visit the pub – had he done so, poachers would have keenly watched him. That would have been a sure way of losing both his job and his house. There were times when the keeper had too many rabbits – they were pests but they were worth a jug of wine. The keeper kept gin traps set in tunnels in the hedgerows. It was his responsibility to visit them daily but it was often left to Dad. The keeper kept a tally of his catches to prove his worth as a keeper. The tails were taken from rats, weasels, stoats etc. The birds of prey had their feet taken. There was rivalry between the keepers to find the most efficient keeper. Sid often went round the tunnels carrying a stick in case any victims were still alive. He knew how to reset and conceal the trap.

'Sid,' the keeper said to him one day, 'something is taking the partridge eggs. Will you help me catch it?' Sid was eager so he was concealed in the hedgerows under the tree. He could see the poisoned egg that the keeper had laid as bait. The keeper had barely disappeared when a carrion crow picked up the egg. The keeper was not happy having to use this method, he much preferred shooting, but when a nest of partridge eggs were stolen he became desperate. His livelihood depended on partridges.

There was always a mutual friendship between farm worker and keeper, each benefited by it. At the close of the shooting season there were often too many cock pheasants left alive. This led to fights and consequently many eggs infertile. He was forced to shoot some of the weaker ones.

What could he do with several dead cocks, out of season? 'If I don't give them to you, I'll have to bury them,' he said. That huge inside pocket which reached from the waist to the bottom of the coat, and from one front right around to the other, has been known to produce more than a magician's hat.

Dad charted and tended each partridge nest that he found. Many hen pheasants were caught and caged so that the eggs could be placed under domestic fowl. This encouraged them to keep laying over a longer period. At the end of the season their eggs became progressively smaller. Such eggs would only produce small birds, too late to be feathered at the start of the shooting season. Small they were but very tasty.

Ma's cooking changed accordingly. Now it was pancakes, cakes, fried eggs, egg custard. Dad liked them raw, or even pickled, and Ma ate them without a guilty feeling.

This annual egg feast induced the children into collecting the necessary ingredients for the wine. Come late April and May it was picking off the heads of dandelions, then the elderflowers, then it was the turn of the cowslips. Ma made many wines. Later in the year it was crab apples and elderberries. There was nothing however that compared with the dandelion; Ma lapped up the praises as the men lapped up the wine.

Each Easter the chapel was decked with flowers, wild flowers collected by energetic children, mostly girls. There were primroses everywhere, every hedgerow, every wood and copse and ditch. Primrose seeds are easily scattered by birds, mostly blackbirds and thrushes. With such a rigorous attack by gamekeepers on birds of prey the smaller songbirds multiplied. Ma had always encouraged her family to pick primroses on Good Friday and this year Sarah and Dora would go. Carrying a square biscuit tin and a reel of gloving thread – this was always in good supply – they headed towards the woods. At the very last moment Sid suggested that he should accompany them. The girls raised their eyebrows, picking flowers was not for boys – least of all Sid. On arrival they soon realised that Sid was in no mood for picking flowers; instead he was searching for bird's nests.

He found a linnet's in the ground on a south-facing slope. He investigated a hole in the bole of an elm and there he found a bumbarrow's (wren's) nest. He had a successful day; just to show he had not forgotten the reason for the trip, he picked an armful of larch twigs. The young larches were a fresh green and their bright pink flowers appealed to him. Sid was pleased to relate all he had seen to his Dad, and he produced his larch twigs when the girls were gloating over their abundance of primroses.

Dad was very thoughtful, and hinted to Sid that he knew a much better way of learning about birds and their habits. 'Everything that has feathers lays eggs in the spring. Then, the female goes broody and sits on the clutch to hatch them. I could borrow you a broody hen; would you like to look after it and hatch some chicks?'

'Oh yes, please,' said Sid, elated. 'I could do that and watch the chicks come out of their shells.'

He went down to the greengrocers to beg an orange box. It had two compartments; maybe he could have two broody hens. He didn't quite know where to put the box. It had to be a quiet place where a hen would not be disturbed. He chose the lavatory. He collected a few handfuls of straw from the rick yard. Ma had another suggestion. 'Why not give the broody hen a few of my guinea fowl eggs? I can spare you six,' she offered. So Dad carried home a broody Rhode Island Red and she was given six guinea fowl eggs.

'Can I have another one?' Sid asked. 'I think there is another one,' Dad said, 'a Light Sussex this time.'

Tom, noticing Sid's enthusiasm, offered a few duck eggs for the next broody. True to his word he came home that evening with nine duck eggs.

Each time one visited the dyke now, one heard a squawk – just saying 'Leave me alone'. Sid was diligent – he removed the hens each morning, watched them while they ate some corn, drank water, then 'did their job'. After ten minutes they were allowed back on their nests. Dad showed Sid how to test the eggs, making sure they were fertile.

Dad explained to Sid that duck eggs take twenty-eight days to incubate, so when he made his early morning visit to the dyke a few days later and was met by the hen with nine ducklings, he could not believe his eyes. 'It's impossible! What was the explanation?'

Sid was soon downstairs when he heard the news: nine strong mottled ducklings – was he pleased! Tom had heard the commotion but was reluctant to show his face. When at last he went to see the ducklings, he just laughed, annoying both Dad and Sid. 'April fool,' he said at last, 'it was April the first when I brought you the eggs. I found them in a willow tree by the stream. The duck had partly incubated them. Now you've got a clutch of mallards.'

Sid didn't mind. He had a healthy family to take care of; he didn't mind what they were as long as the hen didn't object.

Sid, expecting a brood of ducks, had already dug a hole in the garden. He would fill it with water each day so that they could splash and poke their bills into the mud. He dug a small portion of garden several times a day and they gobbled up the worms. The hen scratched in the dust and called the ducklings to feed, but her effort went unheeded. She was a good mother, very willing to allow them under her wings for warmth and protection. Sid was delighted with his brood but Dad knew that they would grow quickly and would soon have to be taken to the lake. To make amends Dad borrowed another broody and brought him two goose eggs.

The guinea fowl eggs hatched, which pleased Ma. She always kept some. Although they were very noisy, they gave her quite a few eggs and required very little attention. They lived mostly on grass and slept on the roof of the cottage at night far away from the foxes.

Sid kept the ducklings until the goslings hatched. The ducklings could now fend for themselves. Sid thought the goslings were the best of all, they were so strong and noble. They also lived on grass. He would take them to feed on the road verge and make his friends envious. Dad's suggestion that they would make good Christmas dinners was ridiculed. Sid knew he would keep them to both lay eggs and breed for years.

Sid enjoyed the spring. He would listen for the cuckoo. With his mates they would catch tadpoles or efts. In the evenings they would walk near the stream to listen for snipe and curlews and sometimes a nightjar.

The boys are home

Several years ago Dad's cousin – then in his teens – worked on the farm. While tedding the hay one day, his horse bolted and poor Ned fell forward into the tedder and he was dragged along, resulting in a head injury. He was taken into the workhouse where he stayed for several months. At last, when released, he had nowhere to go. His brain was affected and he was not wanted. So Ned, like many others, tramped for the rest of his life. Workhouses were allowed to give tramps an evening meal and a bed but not on consecutive nights: he stayed in Woodstock and Chipping Norton on alternate nights. This gave him a ten-mile walk each day.

The only relief from this monotony was when the thrasher was on the local farms. More labourers were needed and he would always offer to take out the chaff. Of all the dirty jobs with thrashing, the chaff was the worst, but it was Ned's way of earning a little money – he was not robust enough either physically or mentally to do anything that needed thought. During this period Ned could be a bit of a nuisance. Dad sometimes found him asleep in the barn. He insisted that he moved on but Ned would only go when Dad had given him his own dinner. Ma would not welcome him at home. He was so dirty, fleas and lice were abundant and the smouldering lavender was always needed when he went.

He spent his whole life in this lonely way until one morning Dad found him in the barn stiff and cold. Such was the life and death of tramps, and there were many of them.

The year was creeping on and yesterday should have brought home the two boys who had been working in the fens with Uncle John. There was no sign of them and Ma was anxious. It was so noticeable that Joe, being a runner, offered to go out and maybe locate them.

It was to be an eventful week – first the boys were expected, then tomorrow it would be the town runners race, the following day was the first flower show of the season. Joe did not hesitate to go in search of his brothers, in spite of the fact that his entries for the show needed last minute attention.

They each tried in turn to console their mother. 'The bunting and flags are already up for the race,' said Sid, 'I hope Tom will do well.' She did not think of Tom. If he did not make it this year, there would be next or the next. She could feel in her bones that the boys being so late was a bad omen. To add to the worries Joe did not get home that night either. Tom needed an early night to be prepared for the morrow. Dad's bees swarmed twice that day so he was pleased.

Joe would not be working the following day. He was looking forward to encouraging his younger brother, especially in the last stages of the race.

It was mid-morning when the contestants were ready for the race. The most important item of equipment was a good strong pair of boots. Some fifty competitors were already assembled and the whole town seemed to be out to cheer their hero. Most wore corduroy trousers, leggings or gaiters. Some had braces in full view, often needlessly supplemented by a belt made of horsehide. Shirtsleeves were rolled up and a collarless shirt was left undone at the neck. Some, not being so rash, had left on their waistcoats. Everyone, however, was wearing a hat – cloth caps, slouch hats, and some were obviously borrowed, large brims which surely would prove to be more of a hindrance than a help. One was left to guess as to what foundation garments they were wearing, but they were there all right. Most of them had already been worn for several days.

Queenie pleaded with her mother to see the start of the race, for Tom's sake. Dad was already there. Ma knew that anyone who had money would be there today, treating his or her friends. She went but was only there a few minutes – her mind wasn't really on the race. After seeing so many entrants, she was sure that Tom's effort would be futile.

Ma and Queenie had just arrived home when in hurried Joe. Breathlessly he explained that the party was only a couple of miles away. It was a much larger party than he had envisaged. Several were returning to the nearby villages.

'Why are they so late? How is George?' Ma spluttered, not giving Joe the necessary time even if he had the breath to answer.

It was a cool, calculated Joe who very sympathetically explained the situation to Ma. George's state of health had not proven capable of the journey – nearly one hundred miles. He had steadied the little contingent of homeward bound buddies, till he had actually collapsed. Uncle John's initiative was called on. He cut two strong ash poles from the hedge. After scrounging a large sack from a farm, he cut holes in the corner of it and slipped the poles through. The stretcher worked. They hoisted George on to their shoulders and walked in step, with a song from the rest to produce the rhythm. The group progressed at a constant though obviously slower pace. Each member of the pathetic procession accepted without question the duty appointed to him. Teamwork was the secret of success and Uncle John as always controlled the organisation. No one ever questioned this. Indeed they counted themselves supremely lucky to have as a leader a man of few words yet endless wisdom. So much could be learnt from such a leader and they were all eager to be taught. 'They looked both ragged and exhausted,' commented Joe. 'But in their hearts, in their voices and even in their eyes it was evident they were nearly home.'

'We are going to play them home,' said Joe. 'The band was ready to go as they had first played at the start of the race.' Joe picked up his cornet and was gone. The 'uniform' of the band was similar to that of the runners. Their library of music was very limited so it came as no surprise when Ma heard them strike up, 'God Bless the Prince of Wales'. As they marched into the distance the sound of the drum lingered after the instruments and melody had faded.

Ma quickly collected her thoughts. 'Run down to the butchers, Queenie, and bring a good joint – mutton or pork or whatever he has got. Make sure you tell him what is happening.'

She made up the fire, pushing the hot embers under the oven. Queenie returned, carrying a newspaper parcel, which she dropped onto the table. 'There you are. It's rump. Mr Whitlock says you're welcome. He'll come up to see the boys.'

It was soon in the oven and the best tablecloth was fetched from the drawer upstairs. A batter pudding was put in the oven as well, as a special treat – there was no shortage of milk since Bluebell had calved.

Ma was showing signs of losing her hold on the situation. 'I can't face it, I can't face it alone,' she said. 'Why isn't Dad here? I expect he's down at the Adam and Eve.' Even as she spoke she could hear the strains of 'God Bless the Prince of Wales' as it crescendoed towards home.

There was much commotion and singing as they approached – the bunting, the band, the holiday and even the expensive meal were all serving a double purpose.

Ma did not go outside to meet them; she couldn't trust her emotional state. She must not be seen to break down in front of friends and neighbours. Much better to busy herself with the cooking she reasoned.

She could not endure the thought of seeing George carried home through the doorway on a stretcher. That was the way he came in, however, preceded by Uncle John. George assured his mother (punctuated by coughs) that he would soon improve now he was home, especially if she had any of her elderberry wine left. Charlie, too, had a slight cough, but he knew he would soon shake it off.

Uncle John admitted to 'a very empty belly'. 'What a good smell of home cooking,' he continued. 'We'll tell all the news when we have eaten. Where's Dad?'

Ma was forced into telling them that he was probably at the Adam and Eve. 'It's runners' day and Tom is running for the first time.'

None of them could believe that Tom had matured to this in such a short space of time.

Queenie expressed her pleasure at hearing their voices again but was shocked at the severity of the cough.

Three excited children ran in full of the joy of town, 'Flags everywhere,' said Sid. 'Yes, left from the jubilee,' suggested Ma. 'And we shall need them again when we have a king on the throne.'

Sarah proudly spread the news, 'Tom is in the first group, we saw them heading for the park gate.'

'How are you all?' said Charlie but before the children could answer, Ma had ushered them outside and informed them that they would be called in for the second sitting.

'Where's Jackie?' said Charlie, 'I didn't see him.'

A sudden silence descended on the family and each knew that Ma would break the silence in her own way.

'Safe in the arms of Jesus.'

A gasp of 'Oh!' Ma clearly did not want to converse on the topic, so she diverted everyone's thoughts and invited them to pull up their chairs. 'Let's sing grace as though we really mean it today.'

As they started singing 'Praise God from Whom all Blessings Flow', the door opened, but, in reverence Dad, Joe and Sarah stood still.

Sarah was getting excited, 'The runners have just gone by again and Tom is still with the leaders.'

Dad greeted the male members of the family with a severe handshake, excusing himself because of the race. He was not drunk but clearly he had been drinking; but each knew better than to mention it.

'I reckon Tom will manage it now,' said Joe with knowledge and experience.

Joe sat down with the family but the urgency of tomorrow's show was demanding his time and he also wanted to support his brother and run the hill for the last time with him. That would encourage him if the finish looked very close.

'Glad you are both home,' he said to his brothers. 'One of you can have my job in the autumn. It's my turn to travel.'

'Oh, don't go to the fens,' Charlie advised. 'The money is good but the conditions are dreadful. Most of the time we were standing in mud and water. No, Joe – don't go.'

'I've already booked my ticket to Canada. I leave Liverpool in early October,' he proudly boasted.

'We'll never see him again,' wailed Ma.

'Don't fret so,' Joe repeated. 'I'll come home again healthy and rich.'

'The future keeps its own secrets,' said Ma. That was one of her frequent remarks. The two boys were surprised at Joe's decision. They thought they had been both lucky and adventurous when they set off for the fens with Uncle John. Joe had refused to accompany them mainly because he had a secure, if badly paid, job. Now Joe was old enough to make up his own mind, and travel without Uncle John. Vancouver was his destination, just about half way round the world.

'It's a case of wealth without health or health without wealth,' said George.

'Unto every one which hath shall be given; and from him that hath not, even that he hath shall be taken away from him. Luke 19:26,' quoted Queenie.

'That's more like our Queenie, still knows her Bible. Can you still recite all the books?' enquired George.

Queenie started, 'Genesis, Exodus, Leviticus, Numbers…'

'Oh no, not now,' interrupted Charlie. 'Let's go outside and cheer home our hero.'

Ma chose to stay in and give the children their meal. George was in no state to go out either.

Dora came in with a large, dry bone that some dog had left in the road. She was always on the look out for bones to sell to the rag and bone man.

'Why do they buy bones?' she asked.

'Bones are made of all the good things eaten by the animal,' said Ma. 'If I boil bones they make a very good stew, and it helps you to grow. If the dry bones are sold to a factory, they get gelatine from them. Then they grind the other part into bone meal. Joe uses it to sprinkle round his roses in the autumn.'

'He offered me a penny to go down the road to collect horse muck in the truck. He wants that for his roses too,' said Dora.

Hearing lots of noise, Sid rushed out to see the end of the race.

In a few moments Joe came in with the news that Tom had come sixth, so he had qualified and everyone would celebrate. Ma was anxious, knowing that he would come in hungry, tired and dirty. He did not come in immediately and Ma's thoughts turned towards Dad. It would be nearly impossible to keep Tom from the pub tonight. Everyone would praise him; Tom had grown up physically today – the consequences were too awful to face.

'A mother can never win,' Ma despaired. 'Some she loses, some spend their money on drink; some, after saving their money, disappear to the other side of the world. We women never get a say in anything. If we ever get a vote we will get things altered. We'll close some of the pubs and we'll stop all wars and we'll help all the workers. But this is useless fantasy; I'll put the teapot on the hob and anyone who comes in is welcome to a cup.'

Would today's events be attributed to the gypsy? Ma couldn't even decide whether they were good or bad. 'The boys were home, Tom had won.' She calculated that it *must* have been a gypsy.

A skeleton in the cupboard

U ncle John's whole life – his character, even his stature – was an enigma. Everyone looked up to him in both senses. He was known by all, yet understood by no one. His mother, Emma, was brought up by her father, as her mother died in childbirth. They eked out an existence however they could. Her father could often be seen doing cellar work at the local pub. At the age of nine she could hold the halter of a horse outside while its owner was quenching his thirst. Now, nearly thirteen, she could unharness a horse, shine its brasses, then, with a little curtsey, say 'Thank you sir' for a few coppers.

So it was that one autumn a carriage drew up at the pub where she worked. She recognised the occupant, an annual visitor on his way to Exmoor for the stag hunt. She knew he was a Lord and he was treated accordingly.

The post had arrived ahead of him, so on entering he was handed his letter. It clearly frustrated him. He paced the room, he drank spirits before eating, and he was distraught. The letter had merely informed him of the arrival of a sixth child and still no son. He blamed his wife. He thought she was selfish – each birth had raised his hopes, only to be dashed. What did a Lord want with six daughters?

Turning to the girl, he said, 'You could do better than that for me. Couldn't you?' She meekly replied, 'Yes, me lord.' That was her usual way of speaking to him, for whatever he wanted, there would be financial reward. She was ignorant of the contents of the letter.

In a flash, he picked her up; she laughed, enjoying it as she did as a child. She became bewildered as he carried her upstairs but she trusted him completely. She was not scared, but she could not understand. Was this real life? Was it revenge? Whatever it was, when she came downstairs she was shaking throughout her body, but in her hand she held a half crown.

'That's your pay, now make doubly sure that it's a boy. If so, you'll get lots more money. I want him called John.'

So it was that John Ashton was born. She collected half-a-crown each week at the pub. She was merely 'a wet nurse' to John but she did not object. It was like being paid to do a most marvellous job. Looking after a baby is the most rewarding work, it gives the most satisfaction. All important decisions in the boy's life were to be made by his 'father'. That word was never uttered; he was spoken of as his 'benefactor'.

He was not a beautiful baby, but strong, large and angular. As a boy he was tall, very quiet and did not mix easily. He was always well dressed and unlike most lads he attended school regularly.

His mother was approached a second time and offered the same reward for the same result. The next one was to be called 'George' but what she did wrong she did not understand. George did not arrive – it was Georgina. The 'benefactor' was not a benefactor, this time he did not even look at the child.

So John and Georgina were brought up together, brother and sister, one in near luxury and one in poverty, one worked hard while the other did nothing. Their mother never married. She did have one more daughter named Kizziah by a different father.

At the age of seventeen John had meningitis and was taken to a private nursing home. After many weeks he went home well again. He had changed; he rarely smiled or even conversed. He appeared to spend all his time thinking. Sometimes he asked questions or even gave orders. His only visitor while in the nursing home was his 'benefactor'. Could he have been told of his origin? As a special treat his benefactor taught him to smoke. 'Always use this,' he said, handing him a cigarette holder. 'Never smoke in front of ladies.'

On recovering from his illness, John was advised not to drink alcohol. He never did – instead he bought a crate of fizzy lemonade each week and drank it at home. He would always share it with family or visitors.

He did not go to church but spent hours at home learning passages from the Bible. He often closed a conversation with a Bible quotation.

Ups and downs

Now the boys had settled at home again, George was given Joe's bed. More truthfully, Joe had insisted that he used it. Tom had recently made himself a mattress with the help of Queenie. It had a sacking cover and it was stuffed with odd snippets of leather. Sometimes too many quirks or gussets were cut for the gloves. Every small bit was used. Some gardeners used their oddments to dig into their allotments as manure. Tom thought his idea much better.

Uncle John had gone to his own home at Freeland. He had bought a house there with a large garden and he lived there with his mother and younger half sister.

As June came in, so did the necessity of a hair wash. So on the first hot day Ma made up the fire with wood and the kettle was ready filled. Using the same versatile enamel bowl, one flannel and the usual cake of soap, everything was ready. The small washing tray placed alongside would serve for rinsing. Water used for hair washing was never changed, but the kettle was kept on the hob so the bowl was topped up as necessary.

Starting with the youngest, one by one, all their heads were washed in the white bowl and rinsed in the tray. After the rinse they were rubbed on that one rough towel, then each sat near the fire till their hair was dry. This meant sitting by a blazing fire on the hottest day of summer. There was never any suggestion of doing it outside. 'You would catch your death of cold.' The boys' hairstyles were very short but the girls' very long.

Ma took complete charge. Everyone went through the ritual, even Dad. Ma was always last. This year Ma had decided that George was in no fit state but Charlie was passed fit enough.

Joe was very busy – his allotment took most of his time. He did not however allow it to interfere with his Christian work. Dad 'sobered up' during the last month, spending more time with his bees. He would soon have plenty of honey sections to sell. Honey was in demand now as it was considered a partial cure for coughs.

Dad and Joe often tended their respective allotments together. They began to understand each other and they were much closer. Dad was really admitting that Joe was a man. Dad explained the details of Bluebell's heifer twins to Joe and he was very interested. Joe felt that a new life, whether animal or human, was God's creation. He was very interested in the Blenheim Spaniels kept by the Duchess.

One of the bitches would whelp soon and Joe was showing genuine interest. When the event started Joe was inquisitive. On this particular day things were not quite straightforward. Joe's thoughts turned to Dad. 'Shall I fetch him?' suggested Joe.

When the Duchess was consulted she insisted that she herself fetched him from the farm and paid the farmer accordingly. So Dad arrived at the palace in the capacity of midwife solely because he had proved himself at Bluebell's confinement.

Dad's effort was successful and the bitch was delivered of six puppies. The last was a rather small bitch. As soon as it arrived the Duchess offered it to Dad. He was overcome with joy. A genuine pedigree bitch, the like of which there were only a few in the world. He would make sure it not only lived, but also thrived. So every morning before work, and every evening after work, Dad could be seen heading for the palace, and needless to say all puppies survived. They were just a litter of healthy, mischievous puppies with turned up noses. He allowed the children to go see them and they were looking forward to the new addition to their family.

Ma was pleased. The whole family was linked by the new addition. She now had a secret worry, but she would confide in no one. Perhaps she was wrong – but could a woman who had experienced the same symptoms eleven times over be wrong the twelfth time? 'Take no thought for the morrow,' Queenie's words kept ringing in her ears.

Dad now had what proved to be an unbreakable link with the palace; he was invaluable to the kennels. He was often given gifts when he delivered puppies. Sometimes half a guinea or even a guinea. He was presented with a dog puppy so that he too might breed these expensive pups. The future for Dad was rosy. Even he began to think that it was a gypsy that had called on Ma.

Sid spent more time on the farm; there were many useful tasks that a capable nine-year-old could do. He was a willing helper both to Dad and the gamekeeper. Dad taught him to climb a tree to snatch a pair of fledgling pigeons from their nest. They made an attractive change to the family diet. He was shown rabbit 'runs' and how to twist wire into snares to catch the rabbits. How to twist a length of barbed wire to locate a rabbit in a hole. He learned how to track moles and catch them, skin them and how to tack their pelts out to dry. Their skins were quite valuable in the winter.

He would walk for miles with the keeper learning about birds of prey and how each one attacks other birds or animals. He learnt about stoats, weasels or any animal that chose the wrong time to show itself; Sid was enjoying life although his mother kept insisting that he was learning nothing. Sid was not interested in reading or writing. Those who could read only read the Bible or sang hymns – he did not want to do either. He was much more concerned with bee-keeping or collecting some larch poles with his father to make a whelping pen that they hoped would be needed next year by the spaniels. Going to school was just a few hours in every day that had to be endured.

Ma knew now that what at first she had only suspected was indeed correct. She had however determined to do her utmost to keep it a secret from all. This was not going to be discussed even after the children had gone to bed. Wearing so many petticoats with so many gathers helped to conceal her ever-increasing problem. She did rest more often, making the excuse that she was sitting with George, or making an extra glove. She very rarely ventured out because neighbours were much more prying and indeed more expert at guessing the truth than one's own family. Although Dad was not frequenting the pub very often now, she could not allow him to hear the gossip when she was not even prepared to tell him herself.

It was the end of June when George was finally laid to rest. The funeral was similar to Jackie's except the bearers were the same lads who had carried him home earlier in the year. They were proud to be chosen. Ma covered up her feelings very well and covered up her secret too. The whole ritual was repeated again with due care and attention. The black clothes were once more placed in a box under the bed.

Bringing in the sheaves

Ma was woken at dawn by the sound of a bellowing heifer. She woke Dad; 'It's that two-year-old from the farm. Isn't it?'

'Yes,' said Dad. 'That's a good sign, I'll be off.' So he jumped into his trousers, picked up his hat and was gone. The sound of a desperate heifer always excited Dad. The farmer had no bull but the heifer when free would put her nose in the air and find her own way to her mate. The walk was about four miles. 'Well worth it,' said Dad. 'After all, that is the only reason for keeping females.'

As he struggled to keep up with the heifer, Dad was already working out when the next calf would be born. 'Next April, I think, just when grass is becoming more plentiful. Bluebell will be dry long before then. Oh dear, that means no milk at the end of winter again.'

'Why did Dad go early today?' Queenie questioned her mother as she felt her way down the stairs. But Ma did not want to be drawn into this conversation. She didn't 'hold' with discussing this topic.

'The heifer was making too much noise during the night, so Dad has gone to quieten it.' She chose her words carefully, intending them to be final. The enlightened Queenie only persisted; 'I expect she wanted the bull.'

Ma was shamed; 'You shouldn't say that Queenie.'

'Why not?' retorted Queenie. 'It's right, isn't it? But why do they always start at dawn? That I don't understand.' Queenie was persisting; she intended to enlarge her understanding of nature.

'None of us understand it all, Queenie, and I hope we never shall.' This time Ma was more successful in putting an end to her embarrassing questions.

The topic turned towards Joe. The local show was the following day, so today he would be very busy. Every vegetable had to be unearthed, washed, scrutinised and the finest specimens only retained. At least fifty per cent would be rejected – they always were. He had apples and plums to pick in the garden and sweet peas and roses on the allotment. 'He deserves all the money he gets,' said Ma, 'I only wish he found a different way of spending it.'

'Talking about money, Ma, what will happen to George's now? What a pity he didn't live to enjoy it!' said Queenie. Guessing that Queenie had something up her sleeve, Ma hedged again before answering; 'I don't want to think about it. I shall do my best to keep Dad's hands off it. I would put it all in the missionary box.'

Queenie had no money, but she was always keen on helping the missionaries. This time however she was not to be diverted, 'Ma,' she said in an apologetic tone, 'I would like a melodium. If I tried hard, I could play the hymns on Sunday evenings. We are going to miss Joe.'

'No promises, Queenie,' Ma answered rather cruelly, but inwardly she was much more sympathetic. It really was a good suggestion and Ma approved, but it would not do at this stage to give Queenie any hope. Dad was probably legally entitled to the money.

The conversation was interrupted by Joe descending the stairs, 'Morning Ma, I'm going to be busy today.'

'Yes Joe, we haven't forgotten,' said Ma. 'How many entries did you decide on?'

'Twenty-six,' came the curt reply. 'And many of them are sure winners. You'll have plenty to cook this weekend.'

As he spoke, Dad opened the door, 'Plenty to cook, did I hear? Well I'm hungry after that long canter. She certainly didn't hang around.'

He sat on the edge of his chair and swallowed a basin of bread and milk with a liberal helping of brown sugar. He was clearly in a hurry. He sat, fully clothed, from his cap to his heavy boots; he even kept his plaited straw bag around his shoulders. This was nothing unusual. 'Why take things off if you intend to go out immediately?'

Orders were going to be given; Ma could always sense when Dad was about to show his importance.

'Will you send some grub up with Dora about four o'clock?' he ordered. 'No need for tea, there's a barrel of cider ready. We shall be scything oats in the top field. Will you come up when you get home from work, Joe? We must muster up every able bodied man we can get. The weather might change.'

'No Dad – that's final – it's my busiest night of the year and you know it. So much depends on tomorrow. I'll come next week. I'll be glad of a bit more money.' Joe's statement carried a feeling of 'I can do as I like now' about it. He had heard 'You can do as you like when you are twenty-one' so frequently, prior to reaching that age, that he had built up an inner desire to 'show them'. No opportunity would be missed and today it was Dad who could not demand his time.

'I'm just going to pick my sweat peas before going to work,' said Joe. 'If I leave them out all day they might get bruised or damaged by the weather. Shall I put them in the wash house?' he asked.

'Yes – put them on the top shelf – then they won't get knocked over,' answered Ma.

'That won't do,' complained Joe. 'If they are put where it is dark, the flowers will bend towards the light and they will be ruined. They must go in the lightest place.'

Sid actually came running downstairs so much earlier than usual, 'I'm coming Dad, I'm coming. I can lay bonds and tie up. You can cut more corn if I do that, can't you Dad?'

'That's right son. I'm right proud of you,' said Dad, patting him on the back.

'If you cut more corn you will get more money. That's right, isn't it Dad?' persisted Sid.

'That's the way it works,' replied Dad, fostering what he thought to be the right attitude to work. The object of Sid's conversation would have to be spelt out more clearly if Dad didn't take the hint. 'How much of that money will I get, Dad?' he asked bluntly.

'Every day you work hard, I'll give you threepence,' said Dad pretending he was over-generous. Then, to make doubly sure there was no misunderstanding, he added, 'When you have worked for one week, you will have enough to buy yourself some new boots.'

The thought of a new pair of boots never worn by anyone else and paid for by his own hard work was a boost to his ego. It would carry him through the week ahead. The thought of being so well paid goaded him on. Never once did it cross his mind that a new pair of boots would ensure he had no reason for not attending school next winter. Oh, what a vicious circle for Sid! Dad had schemed so well – Sid would work to buy his own boots. Even if he didn't work, new boots each winter were vital. Dad couldn't lose, but in blissful ignorance Sid thought he was the winner.

The oats were not really quite ripe but it was much better to cut them while the straw was still green. By doing this the straw would become tough rather than brittle and so prevent the jags from falling off when it was carried. The earlier in the year it was cut, the longer were the daylight hours. Oats were the most difficult corn to harvest as they contained more chaff. They were a great necessity to the farmer as they provided the best animal food, particularly for horses.

'Can I help with the harvest, Ma?' pleaded Queenie. Never would she get this permission. Scythes were long tools and such poor eyesight did not easily judge the distance they reached. The men took great pride in cutting the corn in perfectly straight wide swathes; to do this it was essential to have the scythes very sharp. Sharpening a scythe was an art in itself.

Dad was obsessed with making sure that all tools that were meant to cut were really sharp. Although he only shaved two or three times a week, he always stropped his cut-throat razor. There was a grinding stone at the farm he could use and on his shelf in the wash house was a steel, a carborundum, a whet stone, several files of different sizes and a small tool to set the teeth of a cross cut saw. So, if you needed your scissors sharpened, a hoe, a knife or an axe, he could and would make it sharp. 'Let the tool do the work,' he oft repeated.

Queenie's consolation was that she could help make some plum jam. The 'Early Rivers' had been picked; the whole family had tucked into a huge washing tray full of them. Their digestive systems, so long deprived, were crying out for fruit – another lesson you quickly learn in a large family is that the first chance you get to eat is often the only chance.

They also had a large bullace tree, which this year was heavy with fruit, so the prospects were good for both wine and jam. They must be as busy as the men.

'What can I do?' asked Dora.

'You can bring the victuals up to us,' Dad butted in. 'Then you can have a picnic with us.' Then addressing Tom, he said, 'Come straight up to the top field when you finish at the factory.' Then in a subdued whisper, partly to prevent it reaching Ma's ears but mostly as an incentive to Tom, he assured him of a goodly supply of cider. Tom did not need that extra incentive – the prospects of extra money alone were sufficient.

'Oh dear! Oh dear!' Ma sighed.

'A drop of cider won't hurt him,' Dad assured her.

'No, it won't, but it will encourage him to drink more,' she snapped.

'I'm a man now, Ma – I'll do a man's work, so I expect to drink like one.' So saying Tom stood up straight to emphasise the point. 'You can do as you like when you are twenty-one.'

Ma was not going to give in easily. 'Lions are strong, Tom, and they only drink water,' she reasoned.

'I'm not a lion!' Tom was laughing at her argument.

'Look at your Uncle Jack – how tall and strong he is and he only drinks tea and a bottle of pop.'

'I'm not Uncle Jack either,' he insisted, 'I want to be like my Dad and that's that.'

Mother, despite her striving, had got nowhere. She knew it, Tom knew it. The men got ready and departed.

The four females worked hard pumping water, getting wood, washing fruit and jars – large earthenware jars that had seen service for many years. Dora sat on the flagged floor with a hammer, taking the kernels from the plum stones. Ma insisted that it was the kernels that gave it the flavour. They all worked hard occasionally viewing their end product. 'Plenty of jam roly-poly this year,' said Dora. Each jar was covered with newspaper and tied down.

Sweated labour

There was a conglomeration of noises in the road, horses' hooves, rattles of tins, but above it all, a sergeant major-like voice shouting 'Rag-a-bone, rag-a-bone'.

Gypsies were welcome; maybe it was her own gypsy. Ma had collected a few things to sell to them. She had a broken cast iron pot, several bones, and two rabbit skins, even if they were rather high.

'Any pegs today?' was the first question from the gypsy. They were always anxious to sell their pegs that they had made sitting under a willow tree the previous evening.

Ma however was bargaining. 'Let's hear how much you offer for my savings,' she said. 'Sixpence,' the gypsy said after viewing and considering. 'Then I'll have three dozen pegs,' she said. As pegs were only one penny per dozen, the gypsy had to hand over threepence – which went against her dealing methods. 'I've got some lovely lace,' she offered, 'Would you like some?'

'No, thank you,' Ma replied. 'My Dora is getting very good and quick in lace making. Aren't you, Dora?'

'Yes,' said Dora. 'But I've got a bone to sell.' The gypsy gave her one halfpenny and Dora was satisfied. She spent it on a ball of crochet cotton. She was making a collar to give to Betty when she came home from service. She needed one to go on her dark dress.

'She won't appreciate it,' said Queenie. 'She'll say she can get a better one at Cape's.'

Charlie struggled back home. 'I can't work,' he said pulling a litter of rabbits from his pockets. Dora counted up to seven.

'Dad took them from a nest. They are about a month old,' he said 'Could you fry them for tea, if you have the time?'

'Of course I will. Sid will love one. Small rabbits do not take long to skin. Maybe I'll dip them in batter.'

Dora was already looking forward to her picnic in the harvest field. They would sit on sheaves and eat those young rabbits dipped in batter.

She would collect some wild flowers, scabious, knapweed, toadflax, and so on. They would help towards her nosegay, which she had entered in the show tomorrow. She would watch the butterflies and bees. If they were right at the top by the spinney she could even climb the old oak. She would even look around for the first blackberries.

She loved walking alone. She could hurry or loiter, she could stop and watch anything she found interesting. She once found a hen partridge sitting on her brood. Today, however, she would collect moss, that springy moss often found growing in the dampest places. Dora – as did the rest of the family – all helped Joe, yet every prize he won helped to take him farther from home.

The jam was finished, the sweet smell telling all the neighbours of the job in hand. The wasps also smelt the jam and there was a continual buzz around the room. All equipment was well and truly licked before being washed. Now a round, red earthenware pan was filled with bullaces to start off the wine.

Everyone worked physically hard in the field that day, each co-operating with the other, not for themselves alone or even for the gaffer but for the whole community which depended so much on the farmer and miller. The boss knew exactly which incentive fitted each individual navvy. This wily, clever organisation resulted in giving the farmer very cheap but experienced labour. The ganger and his squad created in themselves a feeling of satisfaction and pride, collective pride. They had unlimited happiness nurtured by toil and sweat and oiled by fermented apples. All strong-armed males in the prime of life were allocated the scythes. Dad wielded the carborundum. But this was exacting work, it was not only the biceps that were tuned for the job, indeed every muscle in the body was tested – it was such work that, over the years, had produced such physiques.

Following in the wake of this manhood came the younger and the older workers with a limited sprinkling of females, all laying bonds and tying up the sheaves. They pulled out a mere handful of corn, placing the ears or the jag together; they then divided the handful of corn and twisted the two bunches together very close to the ears. The bond was now long enough to stretch around a considerable sheaf of corn. After laying the corn straight on the bond they pulled the two ends tightly and twisted them together so forming a sheaf. They were shocked together wigwam style.

The shocks were placed in straight rows to facilitate the carrying. Oats were difficult to dry. The shocks or stooks needed turning if the weather was wet or humid. Wheat and barley were much easier to harvest so shocks were much longer – the heavier the crop the longer the shocks, looking like long tunnels. This was no easy job; the stubble scratched around the legs and the strong straw combined with the barley awns and the prevalent thistles scratched the arms until they were sore and bleeding. It took a long while to extricate all the thistles from your hands.

Immediately one field was shocked the next was started and there was no pause unless there was a field ready for carrying. Cutting sometimes took place in early morning and late evening while the hottest hours were used for carrying the corn to the rickyard.

Building the ricks was a responsible job, often undertaken by the farmer. Each sheaf had to be laid correctly, firstly to make sure that no rain could seep into the stack, and secondly to make sure that no sheaf slipped after being placed. To ensure this the centre of the rick was kept higher than the perimeter and the butt ends of the sheaves were facing the elements.

Autumn celebrations

This year was no ordinary year either for Ma or Dad. Ma was still being very successful in hiding her secret and she intended to keep it that way, but she had increasing difficulty in keeping up her stamina. Dad's connections with the palace were both pleasant and beneficial. Ma thought it would be the ruin of him. She was convinced that whisky would be his downfall.

Dad proved to be a dark horse; any guineas that came his way were being secretly stored. Like the red squirrels in the park he was piling up his cache for winter. His ideas and ambitions would be kept to himself – he too was very shrewd. No matter how busy the farmer was, Dad would not neglect the bitches and litters at the palace and his own breeding pair were being fed and cared for better than his own offspring.

The flower show came and Joe did as well or better than expected. He counted his firsts, seconds and thirds and had secured enough money to finish paying for his boat ticket. Even Dora had a first for her wild flowers, which meant she was the proud owner of a whole shilling. No member of the family went to the show as each had a more important occupation. Ma concocted a plausible excuse. Joe received praises for his efforts and a cup for collecting the most prizes in the show.

The beginning of August brought the annual Sunday School treat. This had been taking place for years with very little variation. Mothers found the time and made the effort in the morning to cut the bread and spread and butter. Ma sent a pot of her newly made jam. The local baker co-operated and allowed the buns and bread to be bought cheaply.

The afternoon started with races: the usual egg and spoon race, sack race and three-legged race. Hoops and skipping ropes were always available. After singing grace they sat down to tea at paper-covered trestle tables. They had brought their own pinafores and mugs, plates were unnecessary; they ate until they were uncomfortably full. The local farmer always offered a field for them to play in after tea. A long plank was placed across a tree trunk to create a seesaw and strong rope was tied to a tree

Hope House was built and used by the owner of a glove factory. Notice the blocked-up windows. The factory (now houses) continues down Hensington Lane to the right.

branch to make a swing. As the sun went down on the day's festivities, they concluded with a toffee scramble. A bag of toffees was tossed over the heads of the children and they all pushed and jostled to collect as many as possible. They returned home with the unanimous opinion that a good time had been had by all.

The harvest days passed slowly by, the days became hotter and each body became more exhausted. Physical tiredness brought on nervous tension, nearly to breaking point. Ma lived each day as it came, trying her best to put family events over which she had no control to the back of her mind. She had no power to change Joe's mind, she could not hope to cure Charlie's cough, Dad drank very little now but Tom appeared to be heading in that direction. In spite of everything, when the chapel preacher called and enquired about the well being of the family, Ma always boasted about the health and happiness of everyone. She did not complain; a good wife and mother never grumbles.

She always looked forward to this time of year; as soon as the first field was carried, she would take the youngest members of the family to start gleaning. This year she must create a plausible reason for altering the routine. She felt that if she undertook the job this year she would 'let the cat out of the bag'. If she did not go gleaning that might produce the same result.

Tom unwittingly gave her the ideal reason. He came in from the glove factory with the news that the factory had procured a very large order from an international sports equipment firm. Every extra pair of skilled hands for these sports gloves would be eagerly taken on. Ma did not usually work for that factory but extra work would be extra money. She was always willing to do 'specials' and now there would be enough 'specials' to last for months. She would save up a little nest egg for the bare necessities that would be required towards the end of the year.

The last few days of the harvest dragged slowly. Both muscle and will power flagged but Dad goaded his family on. He coaxed, he rewarded, he praised and he threatened, and they all persevered to the bitter end. There was the extra incentive of harvest home supper. The actual supper was held in the barn. This mostly consisted of bread and beef, large lumps of rump and silverside with a generous supply of beer, good, strong, wholesome beer made from last year's barley. The farmer made his usual speech thanking them all for their work. All females and children were expected to leave immediately, after collecting any leftovers, the crusts of bread, but most of all the dripping.

To the real old stagers the night was just beginning, with singing and drinking. The more they sang the more they drank and the more they drank the more they sang. This had gone on for so many years that each individual's choice was known by all. There was one item that each had perfected for this type of social gathering. Dad always recited a monologue. It was expected of him – they laughed and clapped in all the right places as if they were hearing it for the first time.

Dad did not stay as long as usual. He was getting older and wiser. Secretly his body could not take as much drink as it used to, even when the beer was free. He was home by ten, but he knew that several of the revellers would be lying on the barn floor till morning. Ma was already in bed; she always went to bed early and trained her family, oft repeating, 'One hour before midnight is better than two after.'

The following Sunday would be the chapel harvest festival and Joe and Queenie were eager to celebrate – that for them would be the true harvest spirit. Joe proudly made the same effort and took great care in giving his best flowers, fruit and vegetables. He was equally as particular in choice as he was for the shows. 'Render unto Caesar the things that are Caesar's and to God the things that are God's.' He often repeated the text, knowing that he could not make either sun or rain – 'I am little use without the help of my maker,' he said meekly.

The younger members of the family were eagerly awaiting the weekend too. It was not exactly the harvest festival, although they liked that enough, but it happened this year to coincide with the fair.

The fair came annually to celebrate the feast of the church although the children failed to see the connection. Joe did not really approve of spending money at the fair. He thought it a complete waste. This year, as he was leaving them all, he promised to give them some money, and supervise the spending. They had never spent money at the fair before; they could not believe their luck.

Dad meanwhile kept counting his money. He still visited the palace daily. His future intentions were purposeful but secret. He calculated that just a small amount could be spent wisely for the benefit of the whole family. So it was that when he arrived home on the day of the fair, under his arm he carried a weaner pig. The children were delighted, as was Ma. This was real progress; it was one rung up the ladder of prosperity. The neighbours would measure them by their stock. They now had some guinea fowl, two goslings, two dogs and a pig. Guinea fowls apart, they all lived in the same room, but there was a vacant dilapidated sty at the bottom of the garden and Dad vowed he would restore it. He would make a nest of straw under the pig-killing stool in the wash house. He would be comfortable there as a porker. Little did that pig know how cruel the world could be.

Sarah, Sid and Dora met Joe and Queenie as they left the harvest service. They were bubbling with the excitement about their new pet so that Joe's pennies seemed rather insignificant. They walked together around the fair, watching others enjoy themselves and each clutching Joe's penny until they had decided the wisest way to spend it. Joe said that each could make his own choice. When, however, they looked at the switch-backs, Joe suggested that money spent there would be wasted, so they went on. They could have two lead squibs to squirt water at their friends and Sid was tempted but once again heeded Joe's advice. There were brandy snaps and sweets. There were coconut shies. One man was shouting, 'A penny a pull. A prize every time.' They stood looking for

Woodstock Town Hall before the shambles were built in. This area had a multitude of uses: storing cattle pens, even sometimes slaughtering animals straight from the market.

some time while children won brooches, beads and marbles. Once again they did not yield to temptation. Large, noisy acetylene flares were burning around each stall; wooden balls were flying at coconuts filling the children with excitement. Some of their friends were sitting on the town hall steps eating 'bread and one'. They looked so happy, obviously enjoying their purchase. 'Bread and one' consisted of a slice of bread rolled around a huge sausage. It must have been the origin of a hot dog.

To spend a penny in this way Joe approved so it was decided by all. They sat down together on the steps and ate their 'Bread and one'. How they enjoyed it! Joe sat down and viewed his brother and sisters knowing that he would be leaving them soon. He looked at the profile of each one. He imprinted their faces in his memory. This night would stay in their memories forever. They had spent their money, they were supremely happy. Then, together, as a family unit, they walked home in the darkness to introduce Joe to their new little runt.

It was a very happy family that night – Dad did not go to the pub as he was so pleased with his purchase and alcohol was now beginning to lose its incentive. Bluebell was still giving quite a lot of milk so feeding it would present no problem for the first few weeks. The dilling was black with a white stripe over his back. He was adorable – he was loved by all – there were plenty of offers to clean up its mess. Who could ever think of a pig as a dirty animal? They are in fact very appealing even if, like many humans, they tend to suffer from greed. 'One of the seven deadly sins,' said Dad, 'but maybe not the worst.' Dad's intentions were to keep it for at least a year, then have a pig feast at the onset of the following winter.

Ma's brain was already working overtime. One red pan must remain empty of wine next autumn. She would need that to pickle the hams. The pig-killing stool would once again be used for its rightful purpose. She would use it also for salting the sides of bacon. Perhaps she could use a washing tray for the chitterlings – washing would have to wait for a few days. The children would have to miss baths for one week. She had nothing large enough to hold the lard, however. She would save up to buy a real lard bowl. She would be proud to own one. Yes – she really was looking forward to making the lard, she had plenty of rosemary in the garden, and it would be the best lard ever tasted.

How they would hang a pig she could not think – but they would, that was certain. With two dogs around it would be very awkward. Dad would probably choose the back door lintel. That would mean that the back door could not be shut for twenty-four hours. Someone would have to be up all night to guard against any stray dogs or cats. Such an event was worth all the inconvenience. It would mean that Ma could give fresh joints of pork to all the pig killing friends and neighbours. In return she would get a joint when their pig was killed.

Having a pig definitely upgraded the family; they were another step up the ladder. That gypsy knew what she was saying – even Dad wondered if it was a genuine gypsy after all.

The children eagerly awaited the event they had often watched in other families with envy. Many times the butcher had joked, 'I'll give you the squeak to take home,' inferring that it was the only thing that could not be made use of. They quite often got the toenails to play with and the bladder to blow up and use as a football.

The following day brought the harvest festival sale. The proceeds would be sent to the missionaries. Joe naturally went, as he was interested to know how much money his items had accumulated. He did not propose buying anything, as he had neither need nor money. The baker had

Mr Gabriel Banbury (who started Banbury's Clothing Store) with his son John. Gabriel's three grandsons can be seen in the far doorway. The shop is in business to this day in Oxford Street.

contributed many 'penny loaves' so, in view of his pending departure, Joe purchased three loaves for the children. Two sections of honey that were sent by Dad were the most sought after items in the sale.

This delighted Dad, re-emphasising his ability in management. He was beginning to grow in confidence, believing that, if given any finance, he was capable of using it wisely. If responsibility should ever come his way he was sure he could handle it equally as well as his brother-in-law. Dad was secretive; he was continually mulling over his ideas. This brooding would put a stamp on his future course of action. When the time came, his scheme would unfold, and there would be no turning back.

A free meal

The early autumn was proving to be the best weather of the year. The shortening days enhanced the power of the sun at noon. The early evenings encouraged the mist to roll up from the low-lying meadows, mingling with the descending smoke from squitch fires that covered the stubbled fields. The wet, lush grass was dotted with clumps of tall, darker green patches, telling one exactly where the horses had chosen to drop their dung in recent years. The extreme of temperature between midday and midnight was beginning to produce the autumnal colours, and indicating to the swallows that it was time to migrate. Its effect was ripening the fruits in both orchard and hedgerows.

Dad enjoyed this time of year. On Saturday evening he would take his ferrets and nets, hoping to get a free Sunday meal. Most of all, this was the time of year for mushrooms. He had looked into those dark green clumps of grass and spotted the first tiny buttons. He walked briskly away from the field. The mushroom crop was eagerly awaited by all, so it was imperative that this awaited windfall be kept secret. Dad waited until the children were actually ascending the stairs that evening. Then, calling them back, he asked for volunteers to pick mushrooms at six o'clock next morning. Such a chance to help out with the family budget could not be missed. Something for nothing tomorrow; the excitement was too great to sleep. Ma found those three versatile biscuit tins, ensuring that nothing would hinder their getaway at dawn. There would be no time for breakfast, not even a cup of tea; they would hope to have time for porridge when, heavily laden, they arrived back home. No thoughts of school, their energetic limbs and minds were too focused on their mission.

The noisy trio left their home in haste, fully expecting to be alone at this hour, but the worst had happened – other children were about. At least one other family would have mushrooms on their menu today. The three gathered pace. First to arrive would be rewarded with the most mushrooms. The grass was wet, very wet, much too wet for their footwear. Without hesitation, off came both shoes and socks, clearly showing unwashed feet, and at top speed they zig-zagged through the beaded gossamer.

Their biscuit tins were soon full – very full. They placed them by the stile that led to the next field. That field was very different. It had until recently been a spinney but the trees had now been felled and a dewpond had been made at the lowest point. There were no dark clumps to encourage the search for mushrooms here. Instead, there were large, dark fairy rings that had miraculously produced huge, tempting fungi overnight.

They were horse mushrooms, tinged with yellow, but the children knew they were edible and Ma would be pleased. 'They are meant for us,' she said, 'just like the manna that was sent from heaven for the Children of Israel.'

Sid put on his footwear and ran back home for the truck as they now had far more than they could possibly carry. Dora walked along the hedgerow, picking large horseradish leaves to place in the bottom of the truck in an attempt to keep their harvest clean.

So it was that this small family oozed with satisfaction as they wended their homeward way. They each carried their own tin and together they pulled and pushed their laden truck home. They knew their mother's face would light up.

Indeed she was pleased, very pleased – but she was also very worried. It was already five minutes past nine. 'We'll stay at home today,' said Sid. 'No,' Ma retorted emphatically. 'If you arrive at school before half past nine, you will only get a late mark on the register.' They quickly swallowed the very stodgy, over-cooked and nearly cold porridge.

Ma selected a few of the best specimens for Sid to offer his headmaster. It wasn't really bribery but Ma knew it would work; it always did. The children helped themselves to one each, peeling it and eating it raw as they hurried along.

There were seventeen late arrivals that day, but the headmaster's gushing thanks made it clear what was expected of late comers.

Ma surveyed her 'manna'. Queenie offered to peel them all. It would be mushroom soup for midday meal, mushrooms on toast for tea.

The large horse mushrooms, many the size of dinner plates, she decided to make into ketchup. It was one way of preserving them for two or three months. The season of mushrooms usually only lasted a week or two, but they would help to fill the larder for winter.

'I shall have to go to the pub for some vinegar,' Ma told Queenie, but although Queenie knew Ma hated going, she did not offer. She would never be seen going to the pub, even for vinegar.

Ma tied a clean apron over the one she was wearing and hurried along the road with a galvanised bucket. She had no other container large enough to hold a gallon. The rest of the day was spent making the ketchup and filling the earthenware jars.

Each day for the next month or two the large stew pot that spent its life on the hob would have a large spoonful of ketchup added, both to supplement the taste and add variation to their diet.

Dad comes off worst

There was one annual task that was always tackled by Dad alone. He never shirked it, neither did he ask any help. He would be spotted digging a large trench in the plot where he had recently dug potatoes. They had a box seat in the lavatory but under the seat was a pit. Each year it had to be emptied.

He started at dusk using a very long handled 'shit spoon'. This took some time: when finished, the seat was re-assembled and the soil replaced over the trench. During the winter months nature helped to filter away the contents of the trench. The ground was not dug again but the following May he would plant marrow seeds all over it. They enjoyed marrows both green and ripe. The ripe ones could be kept into winter, the seeds from the best ones were used to plant. By the following year this plot was back as part of the garden again.

October was a very busy month. The pheasant shoot started in the first week. All able-bodied men who could be recruited could work on Saturday and often on Monday. The beaters massed early in the morning. They were issued with a white coat and a bottle of beer and carried a strong stick and enough food to last the day. A few boys were allowed to help and were paid for doing so. This year Sid was permitted and he was elated. He would walk with the men. They were placed in a long chain and strung out in a large semi-circle around the selected woods and fields. The flanks would nearly stand still while the centre demanded more trudging over the rough terrain. Each beater banged the trees with his stick and shouted, as the pheasants were disturbed. Any game that happened to expose itself to the guns received the identical treatment.

Partridges, woodcock, snipe, hares, rabbits or even foxes: if they confronted the guns, they were committing suicide.

As they trudged along the keeper kept up conversation with Sid – they were colleagues for today. Sid knew him well but today was the keeper's test, he was on trial. The more pheasants that presented themselves to the guns, the more likely the keeper was to retain both his job and his house for the following year. 'Sid,' he said, 'I've got a riddle for you. Up goes a pound, bang goes a penny and down comes half-a-crown.'

This kept Sid thinking all day, but he found no answer and the keeper was in no mood to enlighten him. 'You can go home and think about it,' he told Sid. 'And if tomorrow you have solved it, I'll give you a reward.'

'What will I get?' he queried. 'I'll allow you to come shooting with me,' he said. 'I've got to shoot any wounded birds left around, so I'll lend you a gun and you can shoot.'

Sid kept repeating the riddle; the prize was much too good to miss. He worried his parents and family when he got home. Sid thought the penny that went bang was a cartridge, and he knew that a pheasant was worth half-a-crown, but how was the pound connected? Not until he was in bed did he think about the cost of rearing a pheasant? Surely it couldn't cost that much. He suggested the idea to Dad in the morning, getting up much earlier than usual. 'Think about it,' said Dad, 'there's the keeper's wages for a year; the beaters must be paid, the horses must be fed and groomed. The guns have to be paid for; the dogs must be fed and cared for. Yes,' said Dad, 'I think you've got the right answer.'

There was no holding Sid. It was only seven-thirty but, if he had left home, school would be impossible. Ma was anxious but Dad couldn't care less. He thought Sid was cunningly clever and this was a quality that would stand him in good stead in the future. He was right. The keeper kept his word. He lent him a gun and off they went. He learned a lot that morning, the first being that shooting was a skill and needed practice. He had no beginner's luck but the keeper gave him a rabbit to take home and he was well satisfied. They had finished and were back at the keeper's lodge by twelve noon.

Sid, using his cunning, thought it was unwise to go home or he may be sent to afternoon school. Instead he walked the long way home which passed the blacksmith's shop. That appealed to Sid, so he decided to watch. Two horses were already tethered ready to be shod. He watched the smith repair the shank of a drag hoe. When it was cooled down in hot water the blacksmith sent Sid to deliver it. Sid watched the carthorses being shod – he was holding them by the halter. The smell of the scorching hooves was buffeted around the shack by the autumnal breeze. He liked that smell; it was part of the country air, part of his heritage. It hit him so suddenly that it made him stop and think. Perhaps he would be a blacksmith one day, but he was still putting keeping first on his list.

'You've been a good help today,' commented the muscle man. 'You can take one of those irons for your mother.' Sid thanked him and chose a strong piece of iron that would span the hob to make the pots and kettle more secure. School being over, he went home with a rabbit and a piece of iron. He knew his mother would be pleased. But, oh dear, she was not appreciative. She had had a visit from the attendance inspector today and she referred him to Dad. 'This is your first warning,' he explained, 'next time action will be taken.' From now on Sid knew that laws were made to be kept. Even Dad was scared, although he had too much pride to allow the family to think so.

The weekend of Joe's departure

It was Saturday – the most important day of the week, as it was pay day. There was usually no money in the house until the men came in about five o'clock, sometimes much later. The shopping list already prepared, the children went out together to shop. Dora was beginning to write now, so Mother dictated all the items she really wanted. Dora wrote hesitatingly, continually asking about her spelling. Sometimes between them they did get the spelling right, but more often the shopkeeper made a knowledge-able guess at what was needed. Ma thought this an adequate way of improving Dora's schooling.

The first two items were always the same. First a peck of flour – this was a measured quantity – a round wooden measure was used. Weight varied with the substance being measured. The children took a square biscuit tin to hold the flour.

Next item was sugar – it was delivered to the shop in large hessian sacks so it had to be weighed into paper bags, but each bag was used so many times that Ma said it knew its way back to the shop. Sugar was cheap but brown unrefined pieces of sugar were much cheaper, so Ma always had a plentiful supply. The children liked it, Ma was liberal with it on porridge and on apple or rhubarb pie, but best of all they liked it in sandwiches. Those families that used it rarely mentioned it because it was only bought if you couldn't afford pure, white, cane sugar. It actually labelled the family and reduced their status.

They always took an empty jam jar for black treacle. It was an earth-enware jam jar and it was filled from a barrel by means of a tap. A large bottle was used for paraffin and this was measured exactly as treacle. A few candles and boxes of matches were added to the order. Half a pound of tea was used. Other items were grate polish, carbolic and white soap, soda, starch, hearth stone, blue for washing, brick dust to clean the knives, brasso, wax polish. Then she added other items she hoped to afford,

Joe seen here wielding his axe, with George Walker (his cousin) and a Mr Williams. Note the multi-purpose bath!

cocoa, cheese, and large juicy unstoned raisins. Then she added dubbin for Dad's boots.

After all this she read and re-read the list, crossing out every item she thought she could manage without. She never crossed out the hearth stone – it was a status symbol: she whitened the doorstep and the windowsills as she reasoned that it gave the neighbours a good impression of her housekeeping. This bill came to about ten shillings, but while one child was at the grocer's another was at the butcher's. This method worked well and budgeting was good unless one member of the family needed shoes.

The butcher knew exactly how Ma allocated her money, so when one of the family entered the door, he started wrapping her parcel. Her choice would be a cow's head, suet and some bones. He wrapped it in newspaper and accepted one shilling. If she had sixpence to spare she would choose scrag end of mutton or shin of beef. If salt was needed, a penny bar was bought at the baker's. They did not use table salt. Ma controlled the use of salt. 'I put salt in everything but jam,' she oft repeated. When Dora queried that she had not put it in the bread pudding she quickly explained that the baker already put it in the bread.

Sid invariably did the carrying from the shop. He took the 'wooding' truck to the grocer's and, when all was packed in, including the paraffin, he would continue to the butcher's. This was quite a heavy truckload, bones or a cow's head or sometimes two sheep's heads were both cumbersome and heavy.

The quantity of sugar purchased varied with the seasons. Far more was used when Ma was making jam or wine and Dad sometimes needed it for his bees.

Saturday morning was always busy. Each child was allocated his or her household chore. Sid's job – if he was at home – was to clean the knives with brick dust. He hated it. He could see no valid reason for doing it. They were always stained again by the next Saturday. These knives were made of beautiful Sheffield steel the brick dust tended to sharpen as well as clean.

They were in fact very sharp. If not, Dad would flick them down on the steel. The children used them and it was never considered a danger. The forks were treated with brick dust too. They were pointed, three-pronged and vicious-looking tools, but they did their intended job. The handles of both knives and forks were made of bone. While Sid was being goaded and cudgelled into his job, Sarah was busy sweeping and scrubbing and leaving traces of white hearth stone everywhere. Ma did any washing that could not be left till 'copper day'. She then filled the lamps and trimmed the wicks.

The grate shone, the flues were clean, shoes were polished, hats brushed, the flags were scrubbed, rugs were shaken and beaten, the table top was scrubbed, the window spotless. This was the day of the week when you flaunted your ability and showed the world that you cared about your home.

But this was the leanest day for food. You literally used every scrap of anything left in the house, unless there had been an unexpected windfall. There was usually a suet pudding – in fact there was one most days, but Saturday's was always predictable. The last of the flour, suet and anything or nothing else. It was kept till Sunday morning. Then as a special treat it was sliced and fried for breakfast. This was regarded as a feast, and with the addition of jam or honey or brown sugar, it created the right frame of mind for a day in chapel.

Saturday afternoon was normally spent 'wooding'. All the children went with Queenie and they enjoyed every minute. They learnt a lot unconsciously about their own environment. They saw how different trees grew in chosen sites, the types of flowers and where you could locate them. They could label any twig, bird feather, leaf or flower bud. They recognised any insect that could creep or fly. The abundance of nature was unlimited but the children grew up with it and absorbed it naturally. No one suggested this was education, which was something apart and valued very little by them. Education was quite different; it was kept within four walls, and best left there according to Sid. It was reading, writing and 'rithmetic and life was happier without it. Dad really believed and supported Sid but laws were a necessary handicap.

The evening meal was usually later on Saturdays, chiefly because the children were shopping. If there were a cow's head or sheep's head in the parcel from the butcher, Ma would take out the brains and wash and fry them. Brains were enjoyed by all, especially on toast, so any stale bread could be used. Brains were far superior in those days because a modern humane gun actually enters the brain, splintering the skull so spoiling the brains. The children's constitutions were protein-starved, so this type of meal was craved and it did much to help their growth and keep up their stamina.

After the meal Queenie and Sarah did the washing up as usual. The white chipped enamel bowl was placed on the table. Hot water came from the kettle with a knob of soda 'as big as a walnut'. An old tin tray that started life as a baker's bread tin was used to drain the crocks. With such a large family the washing up did not take too long as they each only used one mug and one plate. Bakers only used flat tins for their cottage loaves or batch cakes.

While the girls were washing up, Ma was filling kettles and pots to get sufficient water for the weekly bath. If you were still attending school you were young enough to be bathed in view of all but, on leaving school, you immediately took on your own toilet. How or when you achieved it, needed initiative. To say the least, amenities were limited. You would have to design a time when that vital bowl was not in use, when you could also bolt the wash house door – the pump was in the wash house and was often needed. Ma found time in the middle of the day. 'I wash down as far as possible and up as far as possible. Poor possible has been missed out again.' The girls were quite particular but no one questioned how the males managed, if they ever did. If the weather was hot it was permitted for the males to swim naked in the river. This was the only time their complete bodies were tickled with water.

Starting with the youngest, Ma personally bathed each child. Although it was bedtime their clean vests, shirts, socks etc. were put on. That was their usual nightwear. There were now only three to suffer this ritual but it was performed as rigorously as ever.

After bath, Ma darned and patched, she sewed on buttons or hooks and eyes. Every threadbare garment was renovated on Saturday night. 'Patch beside patch is honourable,' she quoted, 'but patch upon patch is abominable.'

Dad was equally busy. He examined every boot and shoe in the household. He added a new sole or heel. Using his bees' wax, he waxed some string for stitching. Sometimes he used steel tips or nails. He prided himself on being a first class cobbler, and it was a considerable help financially to the family. He was often called on to repair or remake items of harness using the same equipment and tools.

Saturday evenings they worked together, with the light of one paraffin lamp. All emergencies were completed and all renovations, repairs and reinforcements to keep their family respectable for the coming week.

Sundays in this and indeed most families were very different. Everything they did was designed to ensure that 'when the roll is called up yonder, they'll be there'. That they sang and re-sang not only because they believed it but because the tune lent itself to lusty singing and created in them a co-operative team spirit. They found singing so refreshing; they were simple people taking a delight in simple pleasures.

They sang 'Were the Whole Realm of Nature Mine'. It was easy to sing it and mean it, because they had so little and were never likely to improve on that status. The only permissible action in the household on Sundays was the preparation of food. Animals had to be fed, but during winter when the horses were stabled their nosebags were filled overnight.

Sunday breakfast was the only meal eaten together. It was usually fried suet pudding, often supplemented by bubble and squeak.

The children arrived at Sunday School for the first time at 10 a.m. It was really a miniature service. They sat just as still and quiet. They even had a sermon with text. They all endured it without any grumbles except Sid; he was utterly bored.

They left Sunday School at precisely ten minutes to eleven, just time to run home and cope with nature and return with Queenie and Joe by eleven o'clock. Until this year Ma and Dad always set a good example by taking them, but it suited Ma not to go this year so Dad took this as a good enough reason for opting out as well.

By the time they arrived home just after noon, their midday meal was ready. It was a good enough meal but varied. The Saturday parcel from the butcher determined the meat course. The cheek of a cow was very sweet. A shin of beef pudding with suet crust, boiled for several hours, was also very tasty.

The older you were the bigger helping you received. Sometimes it was backbone of pig; Ma cut it into joints and rolled each joint in suet crust, somewhat resembling a large dumpling. This way you poked at your allocation, dislodging scraps of crust and meat simultaneously – fingers were used, as they proved the most efficient. The stock left in the pot was added to for several days. After the meal was eaten and washing up done, a special Sunday cloth covered the table. It was a woven material. It had tassels matching the mantelpiece valance. The new peg rug was put by the fire – the adults dozed – or read the Bible. The children went back to Sunday School. They arrived back home for the afternoon tea at four o'clock.

This was the time for the arrival of 'Fair Rosamund' from Oxford. Most of the girls in domestic service had a free half-day on alternate Sundays. This was a good chance to go home and they were eagerly awaited. The family was keen to see them and they were often quite home sick.

Even on Sundays there was no butter but you could ring the changes with jam, honey, dripping or lard. Sometimes Ma had made a dough cake, which the baker had cooked.

Betty was expected – everyone would say how she had grown. Her hairstyle had changed to suit her employer. Her hands were showing signs of hard work and too much soda water. She carried her case, which contained one or two garments that needed laundry. There were also one or two discarded items that could be valuable possessions to a poor family. She saved every newspaper, every postage stamp, fag cards for Sid, pins and needles from purchases as farthing change, some bones for the dog, a huge lump of dripping, several old garments Queenie could use for patchwork quilts or rugs. The opening of that case was eagerly awaited.

Sunday tea was no quiet affair. Everyone talked and listened. Betty was brought up to date with family news, and she likewise spoke of her long

The 'Fair Rosamund', seen here at Chipping Norton station.

hours at work. The next service was not until six o'clock and there was ample time to talk and listen. Even during harvest there was never any work performed. On Sundays it was never even considered.

On this particular Sunday a cloud was hanging over the household. Joe would be leaving early on the following Saturday. The agent at the palace had offered him an extra one shilling and sixpence to stay but he had refused. Today would be the last time he would see Betty and there was a heavy feeling being submerged and controlled by each of them. They would all go to chapel this evening and sing, 'God be with you till we meet again'. They knew it would happen, as it had happened to other families. It was as if they wanted to persecute themselves – be martyrs in the cause. It was the penalty for choosing a new way of life. Their characters grew stronger because they did not opt out of a situation.

So it was that the complete family went to chapel – except Charlie who was coughing too much. Joe actually played the hymns and the preacher openly prayed for him. Tears were on many cheeks, Joe was very popular, and his pioneering spirit was praised. Ma and Betty went home immediately after service. Betty gave Joe a quick kiss and left hurriedly to prevent the tears from rolling downs her cheeks. All the rest stayed to sing hymns and Joe was privileged to choose them all. His melodium sounded as never before. They sang, 'The sun that bids us rest is waking / Our brethren 'neath the Western sky'. They finished with 'Abide with me'. Never before had the words meant so much. Joe said his individual farewells to all, promising to take 'The Word' to the other end of the world. He would help to build the chapel out there and teach the Bible.

Joe was often thinking about his own future – he wanted a stable family life. Dad often advised him to choose a girl who was a good cook, which was his first priority. Joe listened but made up his own mind; his idea of necessary virtues was very different.

The first attribute was a strong faith – preferably non-conformist. He was prepared to give a lot to life and he expected the same from his partner. The second attribute was that she be sympathetic, tolerant and considerate towards her own parents and younger brothers and sisters. Next she must be healthy and strong and have the ability to work. Then there would be her qualities as a cook.

'Good looks, beauty, sex. Let's get the basics right.' Joe inwardly chastised himself for allowing such thoughts or even suggesting that such topics mattered. He was ashamed.

The ensuing week would weigh heavy on his shoulders. He never even considered looking back. His character ensured that with any decisions, he made up his mind and carried out the action simultaneously. He did

Joe playing his melodium, with George Walker (left) and Mr Williams.

mull over all the likely and unlikely events that could happen. The North Atlantic was a large, cold, uninviting grave that had claimed hundreds of victims. 'That's no way to approach the voyage,' he said to himself. 'Many thousands have successfully crossed it, ventured into the unknown and returned happy, healthy and financially better off.'

He was due to set sail from Liverpool next Monday morning, which meant leaving Hanborough station at half past seven on Saturday morning.

The whole family and friends were talking of rising early to trek to Hanborough to give him a last wave. Ma had different thoughts. No way would she attempt it. She would take no risks at the moment. The last thing she wanted was suspicions that would ruin Joe's memory of home.

Joe packed two large trunks with his and other people's belongings. One had a large label stating clearly that it was 'Not wanted on voyage'. It contained his melodium, many hymn books and Bibles, in fact enough to supply a whole new chapel.

There were several mouth organs, many new shirts, trousers etc. for mates that had been there for some months. One pal had sent the money to be spent on the luxury of a camera – what a different world they must be living in!

The other, smaller trunk was intended for his personal belongings, but whatever he found, he could barely cover the bottom of it. He put his Sunday clothes in first; then he decided they were the only clothes he possessed that were presentable for travelling, so he thought he had better relax the rules and wear them although it wasn't Sunday. So, in went his working boots, two new pairs of Ma's hand-knitted socks, his working corduroys, one pair of keeper's reject breeches, one new flat cap and one change of underclothes. He had also had two new shirts made from Oxford shirting – they were a present from Uncle John. 'You'd better take these,' said Ma, giving him some darning wool, a reel of gloving thread and a packet of needles. On the morning of his departure he added his shaving brush, a stick of shaving soap and his cut throat razor. The only other necessity was fifty pounds in cash. No pauper was allowed to enter Canada. His uncle had loaned him the money and he would return it as soon as he arrived.

The week dragged slowly by. Each in their own way helped Joe. It was a traumatic ordeal – made worse by the state of health of others when they had come home. They all considered Joe was doing the wrong thing for himself. He was being plunged into the unknown for the benefit of all or no one. Joe had a pioneering, adventurous spirit. Even so he sometimes felt like a selfish brute, sometimes more like a hero or a martyr. Many times during that week he called on his Maker for guidance and he was certain that it was this inner security and grace that kept him thinking logically.

Saturday morning arrived and the whole family was up by four. Ma stated emphatically that she would stay home with Charlie whose health was deteriorating – everyone else was ready and willing to help. Dad had borrowed a sack cart from the farm to take the heavy trunk. Queenie's wooding truck was used for the lighter one. Dad was inwardly very proud of Joe. He has his life planned, yes; he knows where he is going. It's the absence of alcohol that keeps his mind straight and narrow. From now on I will take a leaf from his book. I know where I'm going too.

It seemed that the entire town had woken early – young and old were crossing the park to Hanborough station. This event would be the talk of the neighbourhood for a very long time. On reaching the station they met four other lads from different local villages all heading for the same destination.

Every vantage point was used, every tree climbed, the bridge was full of well wishers, each small child was shouldered so that the hour would never be forgotten. Tears and sobs mingled with coughs and laughs. No one attempted to control their feelings. All the local teenage girls were there knowing that the top name from their eligible list was disappearing from them. Wet kisses were interchanged – most of all Queenie, but Dad gave him a strong, rigid hand shake, wished him well, and pressed a golden guinea into the palm of his hand. At this point Joe was overcome. In his heart he knew their love was mutual. They were in fact each fighting identical battles in different ways. Doors were slamming, the whistle was blowing, the light was green and Joe was puffing his way from them. They stood and waved long after the train was out of sight.

Slowly it sank into the hearts of all that he was gone – maybe forever. As they wound their way back home, the only topic was Joe. To them all, he was the best, he was admired, he was on a pedestal. No one would ever compare with Joe, that was unanimous. They were already talking of him in the past as if he no longer existed. He was out of their lives, they feared forever.

Queenie lands a job

Queenie had been very quiet all the week. She would miss Joe more than most. He was always so considerate towards her. He had so often acted as her 'guide dog' but, in spite of this, she determined to live her life as she always had. She had her 'Rock of Ages'.

So it was that soon after they had all returned from Hanborough station on that eventful day, the postman arrived with a telegram. 'It's a long way Queenie. Can you go as far as Eynsham?' Queenie grabbed at the chance – it meant retracing her footsteps past Hanborough station, then taking a footpath across the fields. Queenie did not hesitate, her heart was heavy and she would love to be alone. She knew very little about the paper mill except that it made fine, thin paper for Bibles. She therefore reasoned that the missionaries would never manage without such a factory.

Even with the strong leg muscles of Queenie, this walk would take an hour. She did not loiter, neither did she hurry. As one booted leg was squelched into the mud, the other snatched out of it.

As she reached the factory, she was met by the owner who enquired if she had seen 'a young varmint' lurking around the walls or heading towards the woods. As Queenie's sight was so poor she explained that she had seen no one. 'He was put here to turn this pulping handle,' he continued, 'but he's a lazy good-for-nothing. He'll get no money this week.'

Queenie handed over the telegram and suggested that she should turn the handle till the lad returned. The man laughed, a strong, heavy laugh. 'A woman can never do a man's work,' he said finally. But while he read the telegram she felt her way over to the handle.

Queenie had always turned the handle of the mangle on washdays. When she helped her Dad at the farm she often turned the chaff cutter or the swede cutter, and butter making was often left to her as the churn handle was rather difficult to turn. Her biceps therefore were more male than female. She started slowly but kept up her pace and it was fully an hour later when the man returned.

'I've never seen a woman work like that afore,' he said. 'How about coming every day? I'll give you six shillings a week for six days. We start at half past seven and finish at five.'

Queenie could not believe her ears; she was being offered a job for the first time in her life. She thought it would always elude her. It was a man's job but physically she could do it.

'Should I ask Ma first? Why? I'm past twenty-one; I can do as I like. If I don't take the job today, tomorrow it will be gone.' She was thinking logically.

'Yes please,' she said. 'I'll start on Monday.'

'You've started today,' he said as he took a shilling from his pocket and gave it to her.

The better she did the job the finer the paper and the more Bibles printed. How the job suited her both in body and spirit. She certainly didn't realise that her wages would be paid from the missionary boxes.

Her heart was light as she made for home, even her boots seemed lighter as she hummed 'The world looks very beautiful'. She had already put the events of the morning to the back of her mind; she wanted to shout her news to every passer by. She muttered to herself, rehearsing how she would tell her mother when she reached home.

This was an experience – indeed a shock – that most of us could never imagine. We expect to either employ or be employed. We strive to find the employment we desire. If we do not succeed, most of us will be sensible and try to be enthusiastic; eventually we will get pleasure and satisfaction.

Queenie had been brought up as a lesser member of the family; health had forced it upon her. Only a few hours before she had tramped four miles tempted by one penny. Both her heart and her boots had been heavy. Her favourite brother had today left family, friends and country to seek his fortune. Many times it had been explained to her that God only expected what he gave.

Light had been denied her; therefore ultimate end products could only be very limited.

She was still clasping the shilling in her hand, spending it any number of times in her mind as she crossed the fields and manoeuvred the stiles and gates. For the first time ever, one penny of hers would go in the missionary box tomorrow. The nearer home she got the quicker her footsteps went. 'Count your blessings' she sang, knowing which blessing would be number one today.

As she lifted the iron latch, all her rehearsals were forgotten. 'I've got a job,' she loudly announced to a very depressed household. Everyone pricked up their ears and listened – not really grasping what this would mean. Ma was trying to cover her disappointment by being very emphatic that she was not physically equipped to walk so far and do a day's work. 'Quite impossible,' said Ma, but even as she said it she knew that Queenie would somehow face the elements and call on the Lord when necessary. 'This job was meant for me,' she insisted. 'Why else was I sent there today?'

The art of living is to grab every opportunity as it reveals itself and clearly this was to be Queenie's policy from now on. She would never be dependant on others any more. 'It's far better to give than to receive,' she quoted. 'No more a parasite for me.'

Ma ascended the stairs that evening in a very disturbed frame of mind. Joe was gone – I shouldn't think we'll ever see him again – poor Charlie is continually coughing – it was futile to keep telling herself that he wouldn't be following his brothers – now Queenie, off to work leaving more jobs for her, just when that active little life inside her was doing its best to be noticed.

What had happened to the gypsy's prediction?

The secret is out

Dad was always happy now. He did not discuss his movements in detail with Ma but he was often at the palace and he often took days off from work to deliver pups or to take bitches for mating. He seldom gave Ma any extra money but she did not question him. He was never the worse for drink, so how he spent his money she could not guess. She calculated that he was saving it. There must be a nest egg somewhere. Dad was shrewd. He had set his sights on a goal. If no one knew his ambitions, no one could even try to dissuade him!

From now on Sarah, Sid and Dora would have more jobs allocated to them. There would not be quite so many mouths to feed, yet money would be coming each week from Queenie. Of course Queenie was working now, so she was entitled to a larger plate of food, that was only right. Ma had always treated her family according to their work.

It was Sid's job to find food for the pig every day, which would be much more difficult now Joe was not there to bring the kitchen waste from the palace. It was beginning to get quite a problem. He begged small potatoes from the allotment holders. They went together with Queenie's truck to collect acorns in the park. Their little pig was growing fast and not quite as welcome in the house.

The pups were easier to manage. Dad put their food ready each day and Dora fed them. There were plenty of bones, trotters, lights etc. that could be bought for pennies at the butchers. The best of the bones were boiled for soup before being passed to the dogs.

November arrived, bringing shorter, darker days with many very dense fogs. Dad was busy hedging and ditching on the farm. His hands were strong but they were also adept when sharpening his slasher. 'Keep it sharp and let the tool do the work,' he said to Sid. He had a very tall hedge to deal with this year, but he tackled it as a challenge. He was always proud of his work and hedging was his favourite task. The finished article was indeed a work of art.

He likened hedging to felling trees. Most of the wood was valuable. He chose a large V-shaped piece to use when thatching for yelming the straw. He selected one or two clothes props for Ma, many bean poles for the garden, pea sticks from the hazel stump, sprays for thatching the ricks. He had promised Tom a decent catapult and Sid a new bow and arrows. Most years he salvaged young briar roots for Joe to graft his roses on, but they would not be needed any more. The small, twiggy pieces he tied together in faggots to use for kindling wood: he could sell some if he had too many. He scraped up the brambles and the debris and burnt it, then stood back and admired his handiwork.

During any free moments they were re-building the old pigsty, a family enterprise, each doing his rightful share. Any materials that could be scrounged were used. There were a few pieces of rusty corrugated iron, kept in place by broken bedsteads. There were two old railway sleepers, and the door was made of wire netting.

Charlie just looked on; his bouts of coughing were more severe and more frequent. He had a fair amount of money he had earned in the fens. It was useless to him now. It was left to Charlie to sanction the use of some of George's money to buy Queenie a melodium. He was certain that George would have approved.

Queenie was now content. Independence was appreciated, her leisure time spent in learning to play hymns on her melodium – she would never be able to read music – but does it matter? she mused. It was trial and error and the family was tolerant, indeed they were appreciative.

It was inevitable – Charlie passed away and was laid to rest by the same lads who had carried his brothers. The family just accepted it – at least the home would be quieter now with no coughing. The weather was appalling. Uncle John suggested that Queenie should stay with them during the week, so shortening her walk to work each day. This appealed to Queenie but she would come home for Sundays.

Queenie actually enjoyed staying at Freeland. Aunt Kizzie was a good cook, but she had better ingredients to cook with than her own mother did. She had an oven in the wall, resembling a baker's oven, and it was used daily. They had one cow, but Kizzie milked it and set the milk in a shallow pan, to take the cream later in the day. Uncle John's likes or dislikes dictated the cooking, as everything in this home. He always praised Kizzie's pastry, so each day she made a large fruit pie, apples in their season, rhubarb in spring, then plums until apples came again. The same dish – yellow with age and baking – was used. When Kizzie had put on the lid, she placed her thumbs together and slowly and deliberately pressed around the edge. This pie was used at midday with cream from the milk. There was one portion left in the dish for John to eat cold at supper-time.

Although John was now about forty-five, his benefactor still met him occasionally in Witney. His boots had always been made for him at the cordwainery; his feet were so large it would have been impossible to buy a pair. His height (six feet six inches) was mostly a handicap. He had to be measured for trousers, he could not stand upright in most of the beamed cottages, and most families did not have a chair large enough for him to be comfortable. He went to the local carpenter and ordered a massive chair.

He did everything at a leisurely pace, with no sense of urgency. He walked to Pinsley Wood during the winter, getting bundles of pea sticks from the hazel stumps. He loved peas and grew rows of them. He bought half a hundredweight of peas intended for cooking. He used as many as he wanted to plant and Kizzie used the rest. She steeped them overnight and used them in the winter.

One day in the wood he found a polecat in a keeper's trap. He killed it and reset the trap. At this time there were very few polecats left, but they were on the blacklist so he did a good job by killing it. As polecats mate for life, he knew there was a female about as well, so the following day he trekked back again and found her in the same trap. He bragged that he had rid the countryside of its worst enemy. He took the corpses home and hung them up by their tails and their noses nearly reached the floor. He invited anyone in the village to come in and see them. 'You'll never see any more in your lifetime,' he said quite truthfully.

Unlike most men who managed to cut each other's hair; he went to the barber's each week. He had both his head and his chin cut very short. It looked like a few days' growth; so he never shaved, nor did his hair ever get brushed.

This was the household into which Queenie came. Gran spent most of her time just sitting in her wicker chair. Kizzie busied herself with milking and looking after hens. The skimmed milk usually went to the pigs. Inside she did very little except cooking. Indeed she was always occupied. There

The author in the enormous chair made for John in 1891 by Charles Mansell of Long Hanborough. Her feet are well off the ground! Mansell lived at the Blenheim estate sawmill. The water wheel that powered the mill in those days is no longer usable, but the beam engine is in steam when the mill is open to the public. The sawmill today makes fences, gates etc. for the estate, and also sells a wide range of products to the public.

was no time for housework. Clothes were seldom washed, the floor was left unswept; food was the main reason for living. They didn't need to go 'wooding', they could afford coal. They didn't need to go for groceries; the grocer called, likewise the butcher. John just ambled around his garden, planting his peas, then erecting wire netting to keep the hens from scratching them up. He could often be seen sitting on the low wall, watching his cow munching the grass at the side of the road, while he smoked one cigarette at the end of his long holder.

He would lean over the wall and watch the village lads playing cricket in the summer and football in the winter. One summer day he noticed what very poor quality, unsprung bats they were using. He walked to Coombe Mill and ordered two good bats from the same carpenter who measured and made his own chair. So, when next he was watching their progress, he called one lad over and, producing the bats, he said, 'Try these out for size.' He was feeling like the benefactor now. There was an unspoken friendship maturing; he was their first supporter. Whichever village team they were playing against, John walked along to watch them.

Dad decided at last that it was time to put in motion his secret intentions. He had been to see the estate agent earlier in the day. He strode home with self-assured, positive determination. As he lifted the latch everyone knew he had news. 'I have bought an acre of land,' he stated. It was more like a proclamation than a statement. They looked at each other. Clearly they had not registered the news. 'I shall not take possession of it until we have found water. I intend to build our own house and leave this tied cottage. I will never, never work for anyone again. I can make a living from one acre easily.'

He had chosen his plot in Long Hanborough, just outside the village on the Witney Road, realising the sub-soil there was gravel – easy to dig – and useful in building. The site was midway between their house and Uncle John's. He knew that John could and would help with planning and measuring. If they could dig through to a clay layer, that would retain water.

The family could not believe it; they had been so poor, suffered so much, now it was suggested that they would have their own house.

Each time he had been rewarded for delivering a dog, Dad had saved the guineas, placing them in a cocoa tin and burying it in the garden. He had now accumulated twenty-five – the exact price of the ground. He buried the money to ensure that he was not tempted to spend it. He had forgotten the taste of whisky, forgotten his pub pals; his mind had been focused solely on his building plans.

He mulled over his dreams, one cow, several pigsties, lots more bees, hens and ducks, perhaps a pony and trap, but most of all a big increase in the number of spaniels.

What a future!

Ma just sat, too overcome to speak. 'I never guessed he had a secret; and I don't think he has guessed mine either.'

Excitement grew in all of them. Queenie was not keen to leave the Woodstock chapel but at least her daily walk to Eynsham would be shorter. 'The farther we are from one chapel, the nearer we are to the next,' She reasoned.

Tom was keen, offering to help all he could, although he would have to walk to work. Sid suggested they should start immediately. 'Do they have a school there?' he asked, hoping the answer would be in the negative.

When the excitement had subsided Dad explained that he really was going to try to find water tomorrow. 'We shall have to dig in the dark, so Sid, we shall be glad if you come and hold the hurricane.' It proved to be a very easy job – they found water at about twelve feet, as Dad had heard – and this knowledge finally convinced him to buy.

Dad set about paying for the plot and fencing it.

It was the wrong time of year to start building but Uncle John would soon be busy with the plans, and Dad sought out the local ganger and bought two loads of railway sleepers. There were enough sleepers to make a cow shed and three pig sties and attached to the end of that building would be the family lavatory. Dad would make a 'party' seat that two could use simultaneously. What a sensible idea!

Joe's letter

December came in very mild. Ma was looking and feeling very pained. She spent many hours pricking gloves, wondering when the event would take place. Would it be before or after Christmas? She had saved some newspapers, storing them under her bed. She had had babies before without an attendant and that was what she decided would happen this time, if she could possibly manage it.

Dad's thoughts and time were directed to the building now. He was digging gravel at one end of the plot – no sense in buying gravel when it was so handy. He went to the wheelwright for a new wheelbarrow wheel, then made his own barrow. He walked with it to Shipton for cement and he collected lime at the Coombe Kiln. John had made the plans and now he was measuring the ground while Tom and Sid were digging the trenches. John had ordered a well head, with a chain and bucket and another handle for Queenie to turn.

Just one week before Christmas everyone was still busy on the plot, when the postman came with a letter. This was an unusual event. Ma was alone, and she eyed it very expectantly. Yes, the postmark was Vancouver, Canada.

She sat down to enjoy the letter. She was a slow reader. She might even have to wait for Dora who was the best reader in the whole family. Joe's spelling wasn't brilliant either although he had been given an old dictionary to take with him. Ma started:

My Dearest Mother, Father and family,
We are all getting on well here; we have felled trees and built our shack on the vacant ground. We are all in work and having good wages. We are making a sewage system for a new town to be called Victoria. What a good idea to make the system before building the town. They do say that the new houses will all have water closets. The folk here must be very rich. We work with all types of people – Japanese, Chinese, French and many more.

The door burst open and in came Sarah and Dora. They all three sat together excitedly deciphering the words.

We can't get porridge here for breakfast, they have a new breakfast food called wheat flakes. We just pour milk over it, it needs no cooking but it is very nice indeed.

The men who arrived here before us have nearly finished building the chapel. It is built of logs exactly like our own shack; there's nothing else to build with here.

We spend our free time sawing logs or sitting outside our shack. I play my melodium while the others gather round and sing. I am sending you photographs taken with the new camera. Sometimes we go fishing. There is a very large Salmon River; we eat them nearly every day. It is the cheapest food to buy. It is extremely good fish.

I shall never forget leaving Liverpool, as the boat pulled out, the Salvation Army band stood on the quay playing 'God be with you till we meet again'.

As for the journey, only the rats on the liner spoiled it. They were running around all night. We were all seasick but it only lasted for the first few days. We saw lots of whales, they were leaping. We saw several icebergs when we entered the St. Lawrence River. We crossed Canada in one train – yes – we even slept in it. We had two engines to take us through the Rockies. We saw many Red Indian camps.

Will you please return the £50 I borrowed from Uncle John? There's £25 I want put into my bank. The other £4 is for you to use. I shall be sending this to you every month. You'll not be short of money ever again.

Have a good Christmas, I shall be thinking of you all, we are a bit homesick, but remember we shall all be singing the same carols at Christmas.

God Bless you all,

I remain

> *Your ever-loving son*
> *Joe*

They were excited and pleased for Joe; indeed they were pleased for the whole family's circumstances seemed to be changing for the better. Joe's letter had relieved the atmosphere in the household. Dad's allotment had produced more potatoes this year. There was a good crop of swedes on the farm and Bluebell was still giving milk. That was for much longer than last year.

The larder shelf was full with plenty of blackberry and apple jam. There were also many bottles of blackberry vinegar that Ma made to stop the coughing, and even if it had not helped this year, the family were still hoping. There were several jars of pickled onions. All this was thanks to Sarah and Dora. Queenie could neither pick blackberries nor peel onions.

This Christmas would be special; Uncle John was coming for the day with his mother and sister. He would order most of the fare. The butcher had bought the prize-winning beast at the Christmas market and John had determined to acquire a joint from it. Two crates of pop were unexpectedly delivered. The females stoned the raisins for the suet pudding. Dad came home with a bundle of holly.

Aunt Kizzie said she would bring her game of ludo. She had bought it last year, but it was viewed with suspicion especially by Joe. He didn't really approve of dice games, so it was taken back to Freeland, but they were now used to the idea: it was not to be considered as wicked any more. Playing cards were different: they were definitely taboo. There were few presents but Uncle John had bought necklaces for the girls and a pocket knife for Sid. There was no alcohol – just plenty of pop – and Sid loved pushing in the marbles.

Betty was coming home for half a day, so Joe apart it would be a family gathering. As a special surprise John had asked the butcher to salt a joint of silverside – Kizzie had boiled it and they took it with them on Christmas morning. 'We'll eat it cold for supper,' he said. 'It will be very tasty with some of those pickled onions.'

Queenie had worked hard with her melodium and she played a few carols, while all the rest sang. Even Tom suggested he should try: what a conversion! 'Yes, Tom,' said Queenie. 'You might be as good as Joe.'

Even with so many absentees this Christmas they unashamedly agreed it was their best Christmas ever and the future was offering so much more.

The unexpected midwife

The children would not start back at school until the New Year but all of them were busy helping on the plot. Queenie had gone back to Freeland as the days were short. Ma cooked and fed the animals at home, waiting expectantly. She was deliberately trying to produce this coming babe with no one in attendance. She had no doubts: she had done it before.

So it was that on the last day of the year, when the whole family were in Hanborough, Ma climbed the stairs. She was convinced of her ability to manage. She wouldn't be in labour for long, she knew exactly what to expect. But after two hours of very little progress she began to lose energy and will power. She was scared, there was no one to turn to, she knew something was wrong. Then, in the stillness, she heard the door latch – she knew the steps and she knew Dad was home. He was actually on his way to Shipton again for more cement, and had called to see his pups.

He listened. He was certain he heard Ma call 'George!' Something was wrong; he knew because she usually called him Dad. In complete ignorance he ascended the stairs. What a scene awaited him. He had never ever been in the room when Ma was in labour before.

He quickly summed up the situation – she was helpless. There was no hesitation. It was obvious what he should do. He had helped Bluebell, he had helped the bitches; now 'the real thing'. Within a few minutes, he had relieved the situation. With the help of Dad she had given birth… to a still-born son.

Nothing was said except one big 'Thank you' from Ma. Were they sorry or were they pleased? They didn't know whether they were experiencing disappointment or happiness. They just accepted the situation as it was.

Dad went downstairs, made the necessary cup of tea and together they drank. Very few words were spoken. Neither really wanted another baby. It was all in a day's work. Dad went on his way.

Ma lay there thinking. Tomorrow will be the start of another year. Had this been the gypsy's doing?

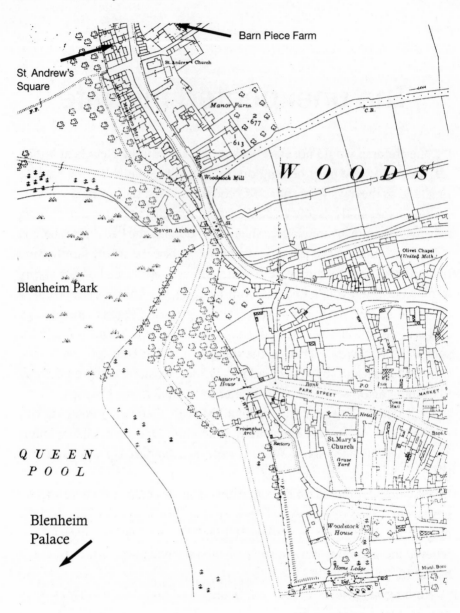

Barn Piece Farm

St Andrew's
Square

Blenheim Park

QUEEN
POOL

Blenheim
Palace

Woodstock just after the First World War

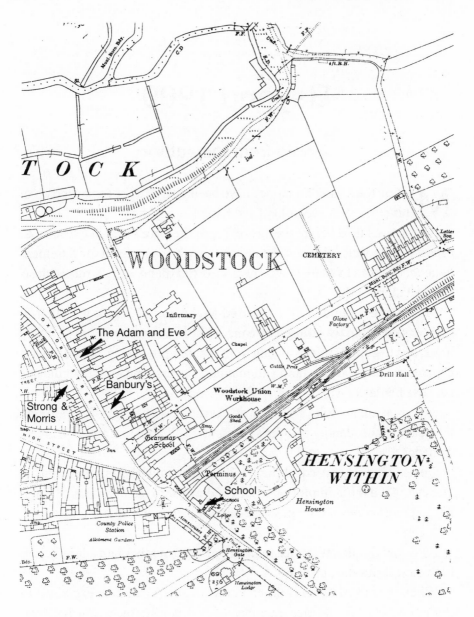

Beyond 1900

A note from the author

Most of the Christian names have been changed for the purposes of this story. Not everyone 'lived happily ever after'.

All the sons died before the age of 21, so the family which expected to become quite well off when the boys were working was in for a tremendous shock. Tom lived till he was nearly 20, Sid till he was 12: tuberculosis claimed them both.

Ma – my grandmother – only lived to the end of January 1901. My mother said death was caused by cancer of the womb, but more probably it was due to complications arising from that last pregnancy. So she did not experience the joy of the family indulging in its first 'pig feast', nor did she ever use her lard dish.

My great uncle John's garden at Freeland is the site of seven new bungalows. The identity of John's true father will remain a mystery, unless someone else chooses to tell *that* story.

Queenie never married – I think today she would be classed as autistic. Her eyesight did not improve but she lived well into her seventies. She and her stepmother never got on, so she left home to live with her Uncle John in Freeland.

Betty and Sarah left service to marry in 1932; neither had a family, and both died about the age of 60.

When she talked to the children in my school, my mother explained to the pupils the life of each member of the family, including her own husband, so they always thought he was part of the family; I have therefore taken writer's licence and included him as if was a member of the family. He is Joe, my mother Dora, and I am the second of their family of four.

The annual race I described was deemed necessary after a train derailment one Christmas Eve. Improved transport and telephones soon made those runners redundant.

The Duchess of Marlborough we meet in the story was a real person, extremely kind and generous. She visited the poorest and delivered many Witney blankets at Christmas.

My grandfather remarried. His second wife's name was Clara. Life for them with their oversized garden was reasonable, and they produced spaniels, pigs, eggs and honey. Then in February 1917 my grandfather hired a pony and trap to go to Witney market. On the return journey, as he came down the hill from North Leigh Common, the shaft of the trap snapped and he pitched forward, breaking his neck. He died a few hours later in the Radcliffe Infirmary in Oxford. He had already succumbed to whisky again. The house he had built stood until the summer of 1998, when it was demolished and two large houses and two bungalows were built on the plot.

My parents, Dora and Joe, married the same year. Dora was 23. They lived in their own cottage in Coombe bought with money Joe had earned in Canada building sewers for the town of Victoria. They rented a small-holding and had fifty-four years of happy married life.

Dora lived to be 95.

D.C.

Glossary

The Jubilee: Queen Victoria celebrated sixty years on the throne in 1897.

The palace and the park. After the successful Battle of Blenheim on the Danube in 1704, the first Duke of Marlborough was give the estate in Woodstock and £500,000, and this has been the home of the Dukes of Marlborough ever since. Only a wall divides the town from the park. The huge, princely palace and the unbelievable landscape by Capability Brown is now enjoyed by thousands of visitors every year.

The **Monument Plain** is a vast area of grass with a tall monument (a measured mile from the palace) topped by a statue of the first Duke. Elm trees were originally planted in battle formation to depict the Battle of Blenheim. Dutch elm disease took them all, and replanting has been with limes.

In 1900 the two classes – the rich and the poor – were very interdependent. The poor needed labour and the Duke needed workmen.

Most of the land and farms for miles around still form part of the estate.

Hames are the iron part of the harness that straddle and protrude above the collar and take all the strain. They serve to guide the reins or hang any other equipment.

A **se'night** is a week ('sevennight').

Cutting the bonds is when one workman stands on the threshing box with a very sharp knife and cuts the string around each sheaf. He is then responsible for **feeding the box**, that is, making sure that the corn enters the box evenly.

A **tedder** is a farm implement for turning hay.

Jags are the loose hanging heads of oats that are covered with chaff.

Awns are the spiky parts of ripe barley, that break off in threshing. They are very prickly and make both the barley and the chaff very difficult to handle.

Yelming is a thatching term. Straw is laid in very straight bundles and laid in a yelmer, a forked piece of wood with each fork perhaps four feet long. When it is full, the two arms are tied together with string, and the thatcher carries it up the ladder on his back. **Sprays** are straight pieces of wood, usually cut from pollarded hazels. Some are twisted in the middle and shaped like staples: these are placed over the straight ones onto the thatch.

Isinglass was a method of preserving eggs for several months. Hens, like all fowl both wild and domesticated, naturally lay eggs in the spring. Their laying period is controlled by hours of daylight and the female becoming broody or moulting. At that time it was nearly impossible to get a new-laid egg in the winter months. Isinglass is a colourless substance with the consistency of golden syrup. After putting it into a bowl and pouring boiling water over it, it was ready to have the eggs placed in it.

Eggs so saved were reduced in value. The yolks were nearly always broken, so they were used for cooking – especially at Christmas. The method became redundant as mains electricity became more wide-spread after the second world war.

People grew a very early **apple** that matured in August. The tree could be reproduced simply by planting the pips. It was a large, yellow, dual-purpose apple and very prolific. Apples were not imported at that time, so these were exceedingly welcome. I don't know its correct name, but we called them 'cat's heads'. They would not keep longer than a few weeks, so many were fed to pigs. I hope they have not been completely eradicated – or indeed the 'early river' plum that ripened in July.

About the Wychwood Press

The Wychwood Press publishes books of local interest, particularly (though not exclusively) of relevance to the area of the Oxfordshire Cotswolds within the medieval royal forest of Wychwood. This is an area loosely bounded by the towns of Witney, Woodstock, Chipping Norton and Burford, and includes Charlbury and the valleys of the Evenlode and Windrush.

We have already published a new edition of John Kibble's *Wychwood Forest and its Border Places*, and Beryl Schumer's *Wychwood: The Evolution of a Wooded Landscape*.

Forthcoming titles will include a re-issue of John Kibble's other works, *Charming Charlbury* and *Charlbury and its Nine Hamlets* (to include Jesse Clifford's *My Reminiscences of Charlbury*, written in 1891-1892: Clifford was headmaster of the British School in Charlbury from 1842 to 1884); *The History of Charlbury* by Lois Hey; an updated and abridged edition of Vernon Watney's rare work, *Cornbury and the Forest of Wychwood*, presently being undertaken by Charles Tyzack; *Walk Humble, My Son*, Eric Moss's memories of growing up in Ascott under Wychwood between 1918 and 1939; a collection of some of the writings and talks of W.D. ('Bill') Campbell, edited by Mary Jackson; and and *The Land of Catavacus*, an account by Dr Tim Copeland of life in Wychwood before, during and after the Roman occupation.

We welcome ideas for further titles, and will be glad to hear your suggestions. We also welcome help with research, particularly collecting oral history that will otherwise be lost. Please write to Jon Carpenter at The Wychwood Press, 2 The Spendlove Centre, Charlbury OX7 3PQ, or phone or fax 01608 811969. We will also be happy to add you to our mailing list for advance information about new titles as they are published.

Thrumming Heart

Paolo Debernardi

Copyright © 2020 by Paolo Debernardi

ISBN (Print) 978-1-914078-10-1
ISBN (eBook) 978-1-914078-11-8
ISBN (Audiobook) 978-1-914078-16-3

Published by PublishingPush.com

CONTENTS

Introduction

“Thrumming Heart” is an English storybook with amazing stories which I am sure the book lover will enjoy reading again and again.

I have never written a story in my mother tongue. It was very difficult at first as the Italian language was still a big influence on my writing, but with a lot of work and dedication, I have managed to overcome this difficulty.

In “Thrumming Heart” the book lover will enjoy discovering different themes: crimes, tragedy, happy endings, sci-fi, fantasy, ghosts, etc.

It is nice to share this remarkable book with other people. Enjoy reading it again and again.

The Author,

Paolo Debernardi

Acknowledgments

I would like to thank Debernardi Publishing and Publishingpush very much. Without their help my book would never have been published professionally and Zizi Iryaspraha Subiyarta who has made an astonishing and gripping cover. I strongly recommend anyone to visit his website pagatana.com.

I would like to recommend Debernardi Publishing and Pushingpush to anyone who wishes to see their work in print. They will look after you like no other publisher.

I would also like to thank Amazon and IngramSpark for the National and International distribution; without them, you would not be able to read this amazing book.

"They always come back, they always come back!"

"It was real," Maggie thundered in the silent kitchen. Brian was puzzled. "What do you mean?"

"I saw your dad one year ago," her voice shivered in harmony with her body.

"You know that's impossible!" Brian shouted.

"I know … I know very well. He died five years ago – but it was him," Maggie replied.

"Nonsense!" Brian exclaimed.

"He came to see me. His gesturing hands, smile, voice. I know it was your dad," Maggie replied.

"I miss him." Her voice broke as her tears fell, "… very much."

"I know mum. I'm sorry," Brian apologized, giving her a handkerchief.

"Don't worry Brian. It's not your fault. Maybe it's better I tell you what happened," Maggie reassured him.

She was shivering more and more, but the more she spoke about it the more there was a sense of relief. A flashback emerged in her memory.

I was reading a book at about ten o'clock when … somebody knocked on the door.

I thought, who could it be at this time? I opened the door and the first thing I saw was a thick fog. It was very strange, thick fog on a summer night. Then a figure appeared out of the fog.

It was an old man. I couldn't describe him very well, because he had a hooded jacket. He was carrying an umbrella.

'Good evening, madam. I am sorry to disturb you. I am a friend of your husband,' the stranger smiled.

'Good evening, Sir. Can I help you?' I replied.

'My name is Mr. Peter Anderson. Your husband knew me very well. We worked together in the same company.' Peter gestured with his hands as he spoke.

'Very strange, my husband never spoke about you. He never kept any secrets from me. Maybe he forgot to tell me about you,' I replied.

I liked Peter, even though I had never met him before.

'Can I come in?' Peter asked.

'Yes, of course, come in,' I gestured.

'Thank you.' We started to speak about my husband, the time of our happiness, you, and the past.

I was very surprised at his interest in my husband and at his gesturing hands.

Despite the lights in the house, I couldn't see his face.

The clock struck midnight.

I couldn't believe the time had gone by so quickly.

Peter apologized. 'I am sorry, but it's too late. I have to go. It was a pleasure to meet you. Bye-bye.'

'Thank you very much for coming. You remind me of all the best memories of my husband. Bye Peter,' my voice was joyful.

I closed the door. His dry umbrella was near my door.

Quickly, I opened the door. 'Sorry, Peter, you forgot your umbrella!' I shouted.

I was shocked. The fog had vanished, and millions of stars were shining in the sky.

'Never mind, tomorrow I'll phone the company and I'll arrange to give him back his umbrella,' I thought.

Closing the door, I switched off the lights before going to bed.

The following morning, I phoned the company.

I was shocked to find out that no Peter Anderson had ever worked there, and Peter's umbrella had vanished like the fog the night before.

I started to believe it was him. It was my husband.

"You see Brian, it was your dad. They always come back, they always come back!"

These final words echoed in their minds and it seems they become stronger and stronger on foggy days whispering in the house: 'They always come back, they always come back!

Waiting

G azing out of the window, Martin was expecting the taxi to arrive. His waiting seemed to last an eternity. The silence in the room was broken only by the thrumming of his heart echoing with the ticking clock.

Unexpected anxieties and doubts concerning Joanne emerged lazily in his mind.

"Perhaps Joanne isn't coming," he murmured.

He was not surprised. She had let him down before on numerous occasions but somehow … somehow, he had thought tonight would be different.

As time passed, his doubts increased, and his patience weakened. Martin began losing hope. He paced the room, stopping occasionally to absently tap his foot on the bare floorboards, his worried face framed in the dirty glass of the upstairs window.

On checking his watch, he saw the appointed time was definitely up. Half-past seven they had agreed to meet and now it was almost eight.

"She's not coming," he mumbled. "Unless she's caught in traffic?" he added as an afterthought, the possibility momentarily raising his spirits. But outside he could see the traffic was light. Rush hour had come and gone. He had to face it; she had let him down again. Would he ever learn?

Depressed, he stared at his feet. He felt he was dying. Then a taxi pulled to a halt across the street. "Hallelujah!" Martin piped. He jumped like a fawn full of life.

His heart was full of joy.

Without hesitation he raced out onto the landing and ran downstairs, taking the steps three at a time heedless of the danger of his breakneck pace.

"Joanne! Joanne, I knew you'd come this time. I knew you wouldn't let me down." But as he drew closer, he could see it wasn't his Joanne at all.

"Sorry, love. I'm not Joanne," the woman said, paying off the taxi driver.

She isn't. She is forty years old. My Joanne is twenty, he thought.

"Sorry," he said, between gasping breaths. "I have you confused."

"Don't worry, love. She'll be soon here. If I were twenty years younger, I would love to be your darling. You seem a nice guy."

"Thanks." I think she will never come tonight, he thought.

"Sorry, love, but I have to go, my family is waiting for me. Bye-bye, love."

"Bye." She was walking away in the opposite direction carrying over-filled shopping bags. She climbed the stairs and entered her house. She was gone, like everybody else in his life.

She is very lucky. She is surrounded by people who will always be there for her!

I'm alone, Martin thought.

Martin glanced down the street and saw the taxi was gone. No cars were driving in the street, no one to meet or speak to. Filled with dismay and disappointment he returned to his room. On the way upstairs, one dogged step at a time as if the entire world was on his shoulders, he reflected that he was truly alone and with a broken heart.

Joanne, the only person he had ever loved, was not coming. He realized she would never come to this house, ever again. He did not blame her though, he blamed himself. He was the one who had been unfaithful, and Joanne had discovered the truth. But he hadn't been able to help himself. The one-night stand had just happened, and he had wanted to explain this to Joanne. He wanted to tell her how stupid he had been and how sorry, but it was too late.

At the memory of the first day when they bumped into each other, Martin sighed deeply. He was wandering carelessly through a narrow street when his eyes met hers. It was love at first sight. He was almost certain it would last and now he had lost her forever.

The thought of growing old alone was unbearable. He could not cope with it.

After jotting a few verses on a piece of paper, he opened a drawer where his gun had been placed. The touch of the cold revolver sent shivers down his spine, but he was determined. He held it tight and pulled the trigger.

Beside his body, there was a poem entitled 'Joanne'.

O Joanne, I miss you so much

our long blonde hair is sunshine

Breaking through a cloudy sky

You always made me smile.

I miss your blue eyes

Mirror of your soul and love for me

But I lost them for one foolish night.

Goodbye to my only beloved.

A Shout for Inspector Wilson

"**O**h! a voice shouted. Immediately, leaving the crossword nearly finished, the butler came out from the kitchen to see what had happened.

Dashing up the stairs, he arrived out of breath on the first floor. He heard footsteps becoming lighter in the distance.

He turned his head to the left and saw the tall figure of a woman running away and disappearing in the dark.

The butler rubbed his eyes; he didn't believe what he had seen.

I think I'm too tired. I need to get some rest, he thought shrugging his shoulders.

Walking straight to the light coming from a bedroom, he recognized the room.

It was Mr. John Smith's bedroom.

Inside the room, Mr. Smith's body was lying face down in a pool of blood on the floor.

Wearing his favourite pyjamas and brown slippers, he was going to bed, but he didn't make it. Poor Mr. Smith! Somebody must have shot him. God, bless his soul, the butler thought.

"Oh, Mr. Anthony. Mr. Smith asked me to bring his newspaper from the living room downstairs, but when I came back, I found him lying on the floor, dead! Poor, man," the maid said, crying. "Mr. Anthony, I hope you believe me. You know how much I respect Mr. Smith. I would never kill him for any reason. He gave me a job. Without his money, my poor family would be dead by now!"

She grasped the gun, not to threaten Mr. Anthony, but to convince him of her innocence.

"I believe you. I know Mrs. Felicity; I know you couldn't have done it. You love everybody," he reassured her.

With great respect, avoiding any contradiction, he said, "Please, put the gun down."

"Yes, Mr. Anthony."

"Oh," he sighed with a sense of relief.

Her hands were shaking as she put the silencer revolver on the floor.

She couldn't have killed Mr. Smith; her hands were too shaky. She also hates weapons.

"Don't worry, Mrs. Felicity, everything will be fine," Mr. Anthony reassured her.

He looked around. Everything was tidy. Except for Mr. Smith's body and a pool of blood on the floor, nothing seemed to be missing.

They regained their composure.

"What do we do now?" Mrs. Felicity asked.

"I am going to phone the police, but don't touch anything," Mr. Anthony replied.

"Oh, no! I touched the gun. I'm in big trouble now, Mr. Anthony, aren't I?"

"You aren't. You didn't commit any crime. Don't worry, Mrs. Felicity. Maybe I know who it was."

"Who, Mr. Anthony?" A lot of questions came into her small but very curious head.

"I can't say. I'm not sure."

Mr. Anthony disappeared for five minutes.

Mrs. Felicity was frightened to stay in the same room where Mr. Smith was lying dead. In her head, voices were whispering 'murder, murder'.

Five minutes was an eternity for her.

Finally, Mr. Anthony came back. "The police are on their way, soon they will be here." She hugged him.

"Don't worry, everything will be fine."

She was very agitated. She was shaking with fear.

"Before I heard voices in my head whispering 'murder, murder'."

"It's only your imagination playing bad tricks."

Silence reigned in the room.

Only the thunder broke it, rolling in the distance and becoming louder as it approached the house.

Black clouds were covering the clear night, hiding it behind their masses.

Thunder crashed above the house with forked lightning.

Mrs. Felicity was trembling like a child.

Mr. Anthony was not frightened.

The thunder reminded him of the bombs falling all over the place in the Second World War. The rain was teeming down, beating on the tiled roof like bullets.

The house lights were flickering on and off.

"Don't be afraid. It's only a bad storm. I'm going to check the electric generator. I'll be back very soon," he reassured her.

"All r-r-right, Mr. Anthony, but don't be s-s-so l-l-long," Mrs. Felicity stammered.

Lightning struck near the house brightening a branch, making her jump.

When it seemed, nothing was going to happen, the doorbell rang.

It was half an hour later. The police are here, Mr. Anthony thought. Coming out of the kitchen, he hurried to unlock the door.

There were two men on the doorstep. One was in his forties with a bristling moustache, wearing a waterproof coat and smoking his pipe. By his side was a youth in his late teens, with short red hair, also wearing a coat, but completely soaked.

14

"Good evening. I'm Inspector Wilson. This is my assistant Constable George Brown. I guess you're the person who called me?"

"Good evening, Inspector Wilson, Constable George Brown. I'm Mr. Anthony, the butler. Please, come in."

"Thank you," they replied.

Mr. Anthony closed the door behind them.

"Can I take your coats, please?" Mr. Anthony asked.

They took off their coats. Mr. Anthony hung them on the hall stand.

"Thank you, Inspector Wilson, for coming tonight. I called you because my master, Mr. John Smith, has been killed. I'm not sure who killed him, but if you and your assistant follow me upstairs, I will explain everything to you."

"All right, Mr. Anthony, show me the way," Inspector Wilson replied.

They walked up the stairs, turned right, and went inside John Smith's bedroom.

Inspector Wilson was very surprised.

He expected the murder room to be in chaos as though there had been a burglary, instead of premeditated homicide.

But the room was tidy. Very strange, Inspector Wilson thought, touching his bristling moustache. I don't understand why the killer didn't set up a burglary.

On the other hand, he could be a beginner.

"Mrs. Felicity, I would like to introduce you to Inspector Wilson and Constable George Brown. She is Mr. John Smith's maid," Mr. Anthony explained.

"Good evening, Sirs."

"Good evening, madam."

Inspector Wilson looked at her.

Mrs. Felicity felt all the attention was on her.

Whatever I say or do, they will never believe me. Even more, maybe they already think I'm guilty, Mrs. Felicity thought, staring at her feet.

She couldn't have killed her master. She is too shocked. She looks like a frightened animal. If she did, why didn't she run away? Why didn't she throw away the gun? Why did she choose instead to leave the gun on the floor? The finger would seem to be pointed at her. No, she's innocent. She's guilty of being in the wrong place, Inspector Wilson thought.

"Sorry, Sir." Constable George Brown interrupted Inspector Wilson's thoughts.

"Mr. John Smith was murdered when he turned his back on the killer."

"There is a deep wound in his back. I believe he was laughing before he was killed because the corners of his mouth are still turned up," *Constable George Brown explained.*

Mr. John Smith knew the killer. It could be a man or a woman. So, when he or she came into his room, something very peculiar happened to make him laugh.

The killer misinterpreted his laugh, thinking he was mocking him. He took out the gun, fired a shot, and ran away. Doesn't make any sense! Inspector Wilson thought.

"Constable George Brown take all the fingerprints in the room and on the gun," Inspector Wilson said.

"All right, Sir. I killed him," Mrs. Felicity shouted.

"Don't be stupid, Mrs. Felicity, you didn't," Mr. Anthony said very angrily.

"Inspector Wilson don't believe Mrs. Felicity. She is too shocked at the moment. She grasped the gun before, not to threaten me, but to convince me of her innocence. It was a moment of weakness," Mr. Anthony explained.

"Don't worry, Mrs. Felicity, I don't believe for one moment you killed your master," Inspector Wilson reassured her.

"Don't you?" she asked.

"No, I don't have any doubts. You are not capable," Inspector Wilson explained.

"Oh," she sighed with a sense of relief.

"Mr. Anthony, can you reconstruct the evening before Mr. John Smith was killed?" Inspector Wilson asked.

"Yes, of course, Inspector Wilson. It was half-past ten. I was doing a crossword in the kitchen when I heard a shout coming from upstairs. I dashed up the stairs to the first floor. I heard footsteps becoming lighter in the distance. I turned my head to the left and saw the figure of a tall woman, running away and disappearing into the dark. I thought it was Mrs. Felicity, but the woman was taller and more athletic. I rubbed my eyes; I couldn't believe what I saw. I thought I was too tired and needed to get some rest. Afterwards, I went into Mr. John Smith's bedroom.

He was lying face down in a pool of blood, wearing his favourite pyjamas and brown slippers. I didn't touch anything, except for the silencer revolver when Mrs. Felicity grasped it. I looked around, but the room was tidy, and nothing seemed to be missing. Then I called you and now here we are," Mr. Anthony explained.

"Thank you, Mr. Anthony. Mrs. Felicity, do you have anything to add to the reconstruction?" Inspector Wilson asked.

"Yes, Inspector Wilson. Mr. Smith was calm and happy when he asked me to bring his newspaper from the living room downstairs. I wish I had been faster returning with it! He could be still alive," she said very sadly.

"Don't be silly, it's not your fault. Maybe then we would have had two corpses, instead of one," Inspector Wilson reassured her.

"Please, Mrs. Felicity, carry on," Inspector Wilson asked.

"I came back after ten minutes and I found him lying on the floor, dead," she replied.

"Did you hear anything or see anybody?" Inspector Wilson asked.

"No, Inspector."

"Thank you. It's very weird, a very difficult case. Mr. Anthony, you told me nothing seems to be missing. Are you sure?"

"Not really."

"Mr. Anthony, did you check the safe?" Mrs. Felicity asked.

"No, did you?"

"No, I don't know the combination," Mrs. Felicity replied.

Mr. Anthony moved a painting. Opening the safe, he was dumbfounded.

"It's missing. Mr. John Smith's will is missing, but who could have stolen it?"

Mr. Anthony said. "Do you know anybody who would be interested in stealing Mr. Smith's will?" Inspector Wilson asked.

"Yes, one person. His son, Mr. Peter Smith. But now he is in London on business. He will be back next week. But he could not possibly be the killer."

Nothing is impossible in life, Inspector Wilson thought.

"Suppose he is guilty, why does he want his father dead?" Inspector Wilson asked. "Because his father hated him. On his death, Mr. Peter Smith doesn't inherit anything. All the properties will be sold, and all the proceeds will be donated to charity," Mr. Anthony explained.

"Ah, I see," Inspector Wilson, replied.

There was a new light in his eyes.

Something was becoming clearer in his mind.

Before it was very cloudy, but now sunshine was breaking through.

"Let me see if I've got it right. If Mr. John Smith dies and his will disappears, his son will inherit everything?"

"I suppose so, Inspector Wilson."

"Mr. Anthony, did you know about this gun?"

"I know Mr. Peter Smith had a similar gun, but he lost it two years ago." "I understand. At the moment I can't prove anything. I need more evidence.

Mr. Anthony, you told me you saw the figure of a tall woman disappearing into the dark. Can you show me the corridor?" Inspector Wilson asked, touching his bristling moustache.

"Yes, Inspector Wilson. Please, gentlemen, follow me. I will show you the way."

They walked out of the room.

In the right-hand corridor, there were no doors on either side, no window at the bottom of the corridor.

How could the killer get out? Inspector Wilson thought.

"Constable George Brown check for hollow walls. There must be a secret panel somewhere."

Constable George Brown started knocking on the walls. After a while, nearly at the end of the corridor, the wall gave an empty sound. On this wall, Inspector Wilson noticed a painting that had been moved from its original position leaving a black mark. He put it back. Suddenly, an opening appeared between the walls.

Mr. Anthony was very surprised. It was completely dark. "Constable George Brown, switch on your torch," Inspector Wilson said. "Mr. Anthony, you stay here, it could be dangerous."

"All right, Inspector Wilson."

The police officers held their guns as they entered the opening.

It was a corridor. Constable George Brown shone his torch everywhere.

Something was shining on the floor. Inspector Wilson picked it up. It was a gold lighter with two initials, P and S, at the bottom.

"Mr. Anthony, it's all clear. Now you can come in."

Mr. Anthony entered. "Mr. Anthony, did you know about this corridor?"

19

"No, Inspector Wilson."

"I see. I wonder where it leads. We're going to find out … We'll be back very soon."

Ten minutes later, they came back.

"Mr. Anthony, I have found other evidence, but at the moment, I will not arrest anybody, because I want to speak to Mr. Peter Smith first."

"All right, Inspector Wilson."

"Mr. Anthony, I would like to ask you a favour."

"Yes, certainly, Inspector Wilson."

"Could you tell Peter Smith I suspect Mrs. Felicity of killing his father? Yes, we know she didn't, but I want him to believe he had got off scot-free."

"Certainly, Inspector Wilson," Mr. Anthony smiled.

"Thank you. We'll be back in a week's time."

Inspector Wilson moved the painting and the opening closed.

The police officers then left the house.

After the shock, Mr. Anthony and Mrs. Felicity went to bed in their respective rooms.

* * *

It was remarkably busy in the house. Mr. Peter Smith was supposed to be coming back after a week, but he turned up a few days later after his dad's death.

He started giving orders to the servants like a general to his soldiers. Mr. Anthony and Mrs. Felicity felt they were puppets in his hands. How they missed their master.

"You're going to have to get a move on if you wish to remain in my service," urged Peter Smith.

"Sorry, Mr. Smith."

"Don't waste time talking. Clean my shoes."

The doorbell rang. "Leave it, open the door! Hurry up! It could be my boss," Mr. Peter smith shouted.

It wasn't his boss. Inspector Wilson and Constable George Brown were at the door. When Mr. Anthony opened it, he felt a sense of relief seeing them. He smiled.

"Who is it?" Mr. Peter Smith asked, truly angry.

"The police are here. Inspector Wilson and Constable George Brown," Mr. Anthony replied.

"Don't stand at the door! Let them in! What an earth are you doing? You are dismissed."

Mr. Anthony walked away, depressed.

"I'm sorry, Inspector Wilson and Constable George Brown, it's extremely difficult to find reliable and efficient servants, nowadays they are so clumsy. Please, forgive him for his rudeness."

"Can I help you, Inspector Wilson?"

"Maybe. As you know, we suspect Mrs. Felicity of killing your father."

"Yes, terrible woman."

"But I suspect another person too."

"Who?"

"Can we speak in private?" Inspector Wilson asked.

"Yes, certainly. We can go to the living room, over there."

They went to the living room and sat on the sofa.

"Would you like a drink?" Mr. Peter Smith asked.

"No, I'm sorry, we can't, we are on duty. Thank you."

"You don't mind if I have one?"

"Oh, no."

Peter Smith prepared a gin and tonic with some ice.

"As a routine, we have to ask you some questions. Do you mind?"

"No, of course not. I'm incredibly happy to help with your inquiries."

"Where were you when your father died?"

"I was in London on business all week. I mean I had intended to stay all week, but when I phoned home two days ago, I was told the tragic news, so I decided to go home."

"I see." Could you give me the telephone number of the hotel?" Inspector Wilson asked.

"I can give you a card from the hotel; there is also the telephone number. But why do you ask? You don't believe I travelled four hundred miles to kill my father.

That would be ridiculous. Everybody knows we didn't have a good relationship, but to think I would kill my father. It is preposterous."

We will see, Inspector Wilson thought.

"Phone my colleague in London. Ask him to check Mr. Peter Smith's alibi," Inspector Wilson whispered to Constable George Brown.

"I'm sorry, gentlemen, I have a duty to attend to. I'll be back shortly."

Constable George Brown left the room.

Peter Smith thought Something is going on, but I don't know what.

"Can I ask you a few more questions?"

"Yes, but I don't see any reason. I told you I was in London on business. I can prove it!"

"Do you have a car?"

"Like everybody else."

"What make of car is it? Is it a luxury car Silver, Mercedes-Benz 300 SL, number plate R756 LYN?"

"Yes, how do you know?"

"A farmer saw your car, on the road after half-past ten, two nights ago."

"It's impossible. I was in London at that time. Maybe the farmer was sniffing drugs or invented something because he is jealous of me? Nobody loves me in this village."

You are walking on thin ice! You were here that night. Your car can prove it. This witness saw your car. He wasn't sniffing drugs or making up a false story.

He's a very reliable person. You are not, Inspector Wilson thought.

"Do you have a silencer revolver?"

"Yes, I had one, but I lost it. I never declared I had lost it."

You're a liar. You never lost it. You were only hiding it in your house, Inspector Wilson thought.

"Did it look like this?"

"Yes, it looks like mine, but obviously, it's not."

"Do you have a lighter? My matches are running out."

Mr. Peter Smith checked in his pocket, but he couldn't find his lighter.

"Are you looking for this lighter?"

"I don't know what you are talking about?"

"Very strange, I thought you were looking for yours."

"Yes, but I remember now, I threw it away last year. I was a smoker, but then I gave up smoking, so I didn't want to keep it, in case I should be tempted to start again. Maybe it's Mr. Anthony's lighter?"

It's a pity he doesn't smoke. How can you explain the marks P and S? It's obvious, it's yours. You try too hard, but you don't convince me. Sooner or later you will make a mistake, Inspector Wilson thought.

"So, what do you think about this homicide, Mr. Smith?"

"I think the killer was very stupid to forget to set up a burglary and to shoot my father in his back."

How could you possibly know these details? I didn't tell you, Inspector Wilson thought.

"Mr. Peter Smith, you have a lot to explain," Constable George Brown said, reentering the living room.

"Inspector Wilson, I don't know what your assistant is talking about? Can you ask him to calm down?"

"No, let him speak."

"Thank you, Sir."

"Apparently, nobody knows anything about your business in London. The manager of the hotel told me it was your holiday. Also, nobody saw you there two nights ago. All the staff on duty over there saw a person who was wearing the same clothes as yours, but they didn't see the face. You booked a room for two nights before your father died. Afterwards, you never came back. I also questioned Mr. Anthony about your phone call. It was not from London but from a hotel in a nearby village. He heard the name of the hotel in the background of the phone call. I checked it and found out you had booked a room for two nights after your father had been killed."

"I don't know what you are talking about! I was in London on business. That is the truth."

"I think I know what happened that night."

"I would like to know as well as you."

"You came here that night, but you couldn't go inside the house wearing your clothes, because you wouldn't have an alibi. In London, your friend wore clothes like yours. Meanwhile, you changed yours and wore women's clothes."

Afterwards, you used the corridor which connected to the outside of the house."

"You waited for the right moment, while Mrs. Felicity was away. You came out from the opening, went straight to your father's bedroom. Your plan was to kill him and steal his will, because if you did that, you inherited the whole of the estate."

"On the other hand, if your father died, all the estate would be sold, and the proceeds would be donated to charity."

24

"When he saw you, he laughed. You couldn't stand his cruel behaviour anymore.

Also, you didn't want to risk anybody seeing you kill your father. So, when he turned his back, you shot him, stole his will, hid yourself until Mrs. Felicity came into the room, and then ran away."

"You have a lot of imagination. You can't prove anything."

"Your alibi is over. All the evidence is pointing to you. The silencer revolver was in your father's bedroom, your father's will disappeared, the lighter was lost in the corridor. The farmer saw your car. Tire marks from your car were left on the road. We took some samples. We have only to match these with your tires and they will prove I am right. And finally, you mentioned the killer shot your father in his back. I didn't tell you this detail."

"All right, I will speak," Peter Smith said, sweating for the first time in his life.

He was no longer in control.

"Before you say something. You are entitled to a solicitor and whatever you say could be used against you in court."

"I killed him. You are quite right, except you don't know why I shot him. I wanted to take my revenge. He used violence on me when I was young. Then I couldn't stand him anymore. He always treated me like a loser. He was rich.

I am poor. I had to kill him to have my rightful inheritance. When I entered his room, he started to laugh and tell me he would never give me any more money.

I depended on his money. So, I took my gun out of my pocket when he turned his back. I shot him. I don't regret it. He deserved it," Peter Smith said showing his wrists.

"You are under arrest, Mr. Peter Smith," Constable George Brown replied, putting handcuffs on his wrists.

Constable George Brown took him in the police car; meanwhile, Inspector Wilson wanted to speak to Mr. Anthony.

"Now what will happen to you and Mrs. Felicity?" Inspector Wilson asked.

"I don't know. We will find another job. We can't stay here, all the estate will be sold," Mr. Anthony replied.

"Take care both of you. All the best."

"Thank you, Inspector Wilson. Goodbye, now."

The Police Car Sped Away.

Mr. Anthony became a gardener and Mrs. Felicity worked as a waitress in a restaurant. Most of the estate was sold, except for the house.

Nobody was interested in buying it.

There was hearsay that something very weird was going on in the house.

Lights were switched on and off, voices were echoing in the house and objects were moving without any possible explanation. But nobody was living there.

Somebody suggested that the house could be haunted.

Some say that John Smith's ghost is laughing because his son killed him and stole his will. Yet, in the end, it was the son who lost everything.

Delta Centauri

I t was 19 June 1994. I remembered it very well like it was yesterday. As my everyday habit, I was jogging after a delicious, but calorific meal, in the park.

The sky was so breath-taking with the moon and stars shining that I stopped running to admire it. The park was silent. It was very peculiar. It was a summer night, so I expected birds to be singing and cicadas shrilling, but that night was completely different from the others. Something was going to happen.

I felt it on my skin. The waiting and spooky atmosphere increased my fears enormously. Goosebumps appeared on my skin. Although I felt uncomfortable, I didn't want to run away. I felt there was a presence reassuring me to stay calm. I took a long breath and my confidence increased.

At that particular moment, a bluish mist came in my direction. I had never seen anything like it. I was sure it didn't belong to our world.

It could be coming from outer space.

Slowly and curiously I started to walk up to the unusual mist. I was frightened, but a voice was whispering telepathically in my head: "Don't be afraid, I won't hurt you."

The mist was very thin and dispersive.

After walking for five minutes, I was delighted and shocked. A metallic triangular flying saucer landed in the park. I had always wished to see a flying saucer closer, but I had never been so lucky until now.

I knew a lot of unidentified flying objects had been sighted all over the world in the past few years and I believed they existed. But it is one thing to have faith, another is seeing in reality.

I rubbed my eyes. I wanted to be sure it wasn't a hallucination or dream. But it wasn't. It was real.

I was so excited, but at the same time terrified. I didn't know what to do.

The aliens could be friends helping us to save our planet or enemies looking for a new world to conquer.

With these doubts in my mind, I watched as a door opened in the front of the spacecraft.

I swallowed my saliva nervously. A tall figure came out from the flying saucer.

Some drops of sweat rolled down my forehead.

He was a medium-built alien wearing a silver suit and gold helmet.

"Don't worry. I'm not dangerous. Please come closer," he spoke telepathically.

"I'm scared, but I don't know why I feel you are sincere and friendly."

"I know. You don't have anything to fear. I come in peace. I want to become your friend."

"Me too."

Approaching him, I felt very calm and all my anxiety was gone.

I felt reassured to see his positive body language. His three-fingered hand showed me the way inside his spacecraft and underneath his gold helmet, I could glimpse a sweet and friendly smile.

Inside the flying saucer, everything looked different from what I had expected from outside. Its external outline gave an impression of a well-defined shape, but I was completely wrong. The inside was completely opposite. The white walls and the long corridors linking the huge rooms gave a sensation of infinity.

In each room, there was a lot of activity. Computer operators from different planets were working together in harmony in a friendly atmosphere; meanwhile, men, women, and children were following other aliens like mine.

I asked him a lot of questions about these operators, but he was vague. He only told me they came from all the planets of the universe.

"You see, your species is very violent and dangerous. We have to select all the human beings we want to contact. You are afraid of us and in your mind, you think we want to conquer your planet. We used to be like you three-hundred years ago. We were extremely aggressive and relentlessly killing any species, but when a superior civilization visited our planet, our society improved. Nowadays on my planet, we live together in harmony and peace.

"With our help, your species will reach the same stage in the future, and maybe you or the next generation won't be surprised to see visitors coming from all over the universe and working and living together," he said.

"How great it will be! New contacts, new friends. I can't wait."

"Be patient, the time hasn't come yet."

He was pleased to hear that I was thrilled at our shared future.

Then my curiosity spoilt everything. Sometimes I wish I could shut my mouth.

I asked him where all the human beings go and at this question, he became very upset.

"You don't have to worry about them. Nothing will happen. We need them for a wonderful project. You see we come for a planet completely different from yours.

On our planet, all the vegetation and water were destroyed by chemical elements.

Fortunately, we survived because we adapted our bodies to the changes. So, we have to wear our suits and helmets to protect us from solar radiation and germs, which can kill us. Without this protection, we can't live on your planet."

"So why can't you change your bodies to adapt to our environment? You have the technology and knowledge. You have already achieved this on your planet."

"We can't. We tried, but we failed. Your body is so complex and evolved we can't succeed. We need your help."

"I'll help you."

We entered a room where there was a black table in the centre. It looked very solid like a stone and it gave me an impression of being cold.

He approached another alien and together they had a brief conversation telepathically.

Then he came back and reassured me.

"Don't be afraid! You will have some tests, but you won't feel any pain or fear."

I undressed as he asked me to and lay on the table completely naked.

The table was exceptionally soft and warm giving me the sensation of being on a bed.

From the wall, a flat machine appeared, scanned my body, and disappeared. It was a very strange sensation, but afterward, I felt all my pain and fear had gone.

I was relaxed.

A long tube came out from the side of the table. It stimulated my male organ and sucked my sperms away.

"We need your sperm to combine human chromosomes with ours. Only in this way will our babies be able to live on your planet in the future."

I felt miserable being treated as a guinea pig. I prefer to make love naturally, instead of artificially. But I couldn't really complain about it. I'd be a father.

The tube disappeared, and a long thin silver tube appeared. It went inside my nose. The operation was brief and was painless. The tube came out from my nose and vanished.

It was all over. He reassured me and allowed me to dress.

"It was for your own good. You had a terrible illness, but my machine removed it. Now I would like to show you where I come from. Please follow me."

"Yes, sure."

I followed him. We entered another room, which was covered by maps of the constellations and galaxies of the universe.

He pointed to a planet.

"I come from Delta Centauri on a planet called 'Ursula'. It is 5 light-years from earth. I come in peace. I want to protect your planet from nuclear self-destruction or a meteorite impact."

He carried on explaining, but my mind was completely full of information. I remembered only that I peered out at another room. There were human children there playing with young aliens.

They were enjoying this so much they were laughing and running around.

Then everything was blank. I don't remember anything. Maybe they removed my experience from my head.

I found myself on the grass in the park. In that particular instant, the only thing I remembered was the bluish mist, not the flying saucer and the following events.

I looked at my watch.

It was 11 o'clock. There were three hours missing. I didn't remember how and where I had spent them.

Not finding any explanation, I decided to go home.

The following morning, I panicked to see drops of blood coming out from my nose. It was very weird. I was so alarmed that I went straight to the hospital where I had a check-up.

The doctor was surprised to find there was a chance of cancer in my head, but now it had gone mysteriously. There was only a strange unidentified piece of metal in my head. I explained to the doctor that I had never been operated on. I didn't know where it had come from.

He suggested going to the psychiatrist because it could be a case of alien abduction.

At first, I was reluctant to go. Who would believe me? They would think I was mad. Then I changed my mind. I was too curious. I wanted to give it a go. I made an appointment.

After several retro-hypnoses, I relived my experience. I couldn't remember it, because it was hidden in my memory. But afterward, it was recalled. I remembered the end of my experience. I was on the grass looking at the spacecraft in the sky, flying away at high speed.

The psychiatrist introduced me to his friend, who was also abducted by aliens, to share my experience with other people.

This is the reason I am here tonight. At last, I would like to say it is a real story. I didn't invent anything. It really happened to me. I know there are many people who deceived others with incredible stories coming from their vivid imaginations. But I'm not like them. This is real life.

Every night I wake up, screaming from this nightmare.

Later that night, the expert thought before writing in a file, "I believe it is a genuine story. The witness is honest, sincere, and objective." Then he put it in a drawer together with hundreds of other files. They all told the same story.

The Incredible Tony

"Help, help," a little girl was screaming in the strong and cold River Ice.

No one seemed to hear her. Petrified, they were staring at her from the riverbank.

Only Tony, standing on the bridge 5 feet above, was ready for action.

In a split second, he jumped from the bridge and dived into the river, heedless of danger.

For a couple of minutes, there was no trace of Tony.

Some women were starting to cry, and others were looking down very depressed as the last hope of rescuing the little girl vanished.

In this moment of despair, Tony appeared on the surface.

The tears of sadness turned into tears of joy.

Some people jumped and cheered him on, and others applauded him.

With powerful strokes, his arms and legs cut through the current of the river like a salmon.

"Don't be afraid, everything will be alright." With calm words, Tony reassured the little girl as he approached her. She sighed with a sense of relief and smiled for the first time.

He put an arm around her. She stopped shivering and looked at him, and he smiled back. He was swimming more slowly, and the journey seemed to be endless.

She was extremely glad to feel the sand of the riverbank where a paramedic was standing by holding a blanket on his arm. The paramedic came close to her, wrapping her with the blanket and drying her hair. The crowd was still applauding and cheering Tony on. He was very calm, and his clothes appeared not to be wet at all.

A forty-year-old woman approached the little girl with anxiety and rage.

"What were you thinking of trying to pick up the ball in the deep water? Did you not know the current of the River Ice is so strong and cold?" the worried woman asked.

"I know mum," the little girl replied between tears.

"I would take it easy on her. She was so frightened," Tony said looking at her mother. His eyes had a brief blue sparkling light.

The anxious woman winked in a way to say thank you. Now she was very calm, and all her worries and aggression were completely gone.

She and her daughter walked home holding hands. The little girl turned her head for the last time and winked at Tony.

Well done Tony! You have rescued that little girl from drowning. You have saved the day again!" the crowd was shouting. "You are our hero!" other people were saying.

"He is just a mad man."

"I agree. Why would he risk his life to save that little girl?"

"He doesn't even know her, and her mother is extremely poor. How could she pay him back?"

Two older men were whispering behind the crowd.

Tony saw them and replied to the crowd.

"I am not a hero. I am an ordinary man who loves helping people. That is who I am."

"Don't be silly Tony. Have you forgotten what you did yesterday?" Constable Ross Chapman asked.

"No, I cannot forget," Tony replied.

Tony is thinking, I am an ordinary man.

In reality, he is extraordinary.

Four-feet-ten-inches tall with wide shoulders, marine biceps, short and firm muscular legs, Tony is very strong as well as agile and fast. Even

34

more unusually, he has a sparkling light in his blue eyes when he helps people in danger. They feel relaxed and calm after they see it.

In his heart he knows he is a friend to everyone and helping people makes him feel so good.

They feel good too and thank him with every kind of present. He always accepts them with a smile.

This is not the first time the inhabitants of his village Ice had seen his acts of heroism. Every single day something terrible happens in the village and Tony always saves the day. His name is always on the lips of people for his bravery and kindness. Nobody can forget what Tony had done the day before.

There was a fire in his friend's house and a baby was in the bedroom. Lucy could not help the baby because the fire was blocking the door. So, she ran out and called for help. The fire brigade was extinguishing another fire in a neighbouring city and therefore they would not arrive in time. Lucy was horrified and shocked.

She was crying, begging people to save her baby. No one came out to rescue her baby except Tony. Without any hesitation, he entered the house that was on fire and ran up the stairs.

A couple of minutes later he walked out with Lucy's baby in his arms.

Both Tony and the baby were unharmed. Lucy was incredibly grateful, and she was smiling, even though her beautiful house had burnt down.

An unusually cold wind was blowing on this hottest day of summer.

Tony waved goodbye to everyone on the riverbank. He felt shivers down his spine. He knew that was a bad sign. It meant something terrible would happen to him and he could not do anything about it. He carried on walking to the entrance of the bank and before he stepped inside, he looked onto the main street.

There was a crowd waving and applauding him by way of saying thank you for rescuing the little girl in the river.

He smiled back with a strange sadness.

Inside the bank, it was very chaotic.

A lot of people were queuing at the counter with payslips and bills. Lucy was there as well. She was so beautiful with her blonde hair tied back and a new red dress up to her knees. She smiled.

In this sweet moment, the door of the bank opened violently, a short man wearing a balaclava thundered into the hall carrying a shining semi-automatic gun and a plastic bag.

Pointing the gun at the crowd, with a distinct husky voice, he thundered:

"Nobody will get hurt if everyone follows my demands!"

"Lie down on the floor, everyone!"

All the people were terrified. Some young children and women were on the floor crying. Others were too frightened to react.

Tony was observing. He did not want to put anyone in danger. He understood the gunman was frantic.

The last thing he wanted was for someone to get hurt.

"Put all the money in the bag," the gunman shouted to the clerk.

"If i were you, i would run. The police will arrive soon, and you will be nicked."

"Shut up! Shut up! If you don't shut up, i'll shoot someone!"

"Lie down on the floor or the young woman beside you will die!"

Lucy was petrified at the thought of being shot.

The gunman's hand was shaking and a drop of sweat rolled down his forehead.

He was losing control of his nerves.

In an insane state of mind, he pulled the trigger of the semi-automatic and a bullet was released.

In a split second, tony put himself between the bullet and lucy. Some people screamed at the shot. The bullet hit his chest.

Lucy stopped tony from falling and then lay his body down on the floor.

"Do not be afraid, everything will be fine," tony reassured lucy with a warm smile.

In the meantime, the sound of police sirens was clearly audible outside. There were a lot of people coming and going.

In this confusion, the gunman saw a chance to escape. He took the money and ran out of the back door, but the police were waiting for him.

Several reply shots were heard, then silence.

Lucy took her courage in both hands and walked out of the bank looking for help.

An ambulance was outside. Two paramedics got out and approached lucy who was very agitated and confused.

"There is a man who has been shot. There is a man who has been shot," lucy was saying repeatedly.

"Show us the way, madam."

Lucy showed them the way into the bank.

She was dumbfounded.

She asked everyone where tony was. No one could tell her. Some said they did not know who he was, while others were still horrified by the terrible experience.

The news of this tragedy spread like wildfire. Everyone was talking about it.

The inhabitants of the neighbouring villages could not believe a man of such bravery and kindness had ever really lived.

They thought he was a fruit of the imagination or a legend told by the inhabitants of the village ice, but all of them knew tony was real and he died doing the thing he loved most, helping people.

Thriller in the Scary Night

L ucy knew she should not have walked in the scary alley. She could not help it. She had finished a very long day at work in the cafeteria and she was not thinking straight.

The narrow alley was filthy with rubbish, dead rats, and decomposed food.

The place stank so badly Lucy felt nauseous.

The police had reported that on many occasions, women had disappeared in the past few years. Someone suggested the abductor was hiding somewhere, ready to strike again, making the alley very unsafe.

All the women would eventually reappear, naked and dead, with cuts and bruises on their bodies. The police found they had been sexually assaulted before being fatally stabbed with a long knife.

Lucy felt extremely uncomfortable walking through the alley. She wanted to go through as quickly as possible. The alley was between old derelict factories, which had not been used for years. So, even if she was in danger and shouting for help, no one would ever come to rescue her.

The alley was very long and there was no way to escape so she had to walk to the other end.

She heard a noise behind her. A light footstep in the distance. She stopped. The noise stopped as well. She began to walk again, and the footsteps were much louder. She started to walk more quickly but the mysterious stranger increased its speed to keep up.

Lucy looked back and said, "Who is there?"

No one replied.

Lucy started to cry and get agitated. She was so frightened. She glanced back and saw a shadow on the wall.

Her walk became a run, but the mysterious stranger did not give up the chase and he began to run faster and faster.

Lucy could feel her heart beating in her chest. Her breath became heavier.

She knew she could not hide anywhere or turn anywhere to escape from the mysterious stranger. She felt she was like an animal in a cage. She glanced back for the third time and now the shadow was bigger. She could see the shadow was holding something in its right hand. She could not make out what it was.

She assumed it was a knife. The metallic blade vibrated in the air making Lucy tremble violently.

The mysterious stranger was gaining on Lucy. She felt her chances of survival were becoming slimmer and slimmer. The mysterious stranger was almost behind her, ready to strike.

Lucy saw the exit of the alley in front of her. Her eyes filled with joy. With her last attempt to survive, she pushed her tired legs to the extreme.

Lucy collided against a body in front of her. She was lying on the floor.

Thinking the mysterious stranger had managed to get in front of her, she began to crawl backward from him.

"Are you OK, madam?" the police officer said with a warm smile.

"I'm fine, thanks," Lucy replied with a relieved smile after catching her breath.

"Please take my hand, I will help you to stand up."

She was so happy to see a police officer in this area. She felt so safe now. She gave him her hand and the police officer helped her.

"Have you walked down the alley?"

"Yes, I did."

"Did you know it is dangerous?"

"Yes, I heard. It was my mistake. Halfway down, I realized I was in the alley.

Have you seen anyone coming out from the alley except me?"

"No madam. Why, did you?"

"I thought someone was chasing me with a knife."

"I can assure you no one came out of the alley except you. Tonight, I am patrolling this area to make it safe."

"I feel safe now. Thanks for being here."

"It is my duty, madam. I hope you have a safe journey."

"Thanks, officer."

Lucy felt better. Even though she had escaped from the danger, she did not feel completely comfortable. There was a weird feeling the mysterious stranger could have followed her. She was walking in the main square where a lot of people were still about. She tried to look at their shadows to see if she could recognize the one that had chased her earlier, but they were absolutely different. Even she tried to smell the air or hear the footsteps. None of them matched her memory.

There was not a trace of the mysterious stranger, but Lucy was still incredibly careful walking along the main street and taking the bus to go home.

She did not want to be off her guard. She was staring at anyone she could see, and the people looked at her in surprise.

She was feeling more confident in herself after she recognized her street. She began to have more strength and she knew no one could harm her now. Her husband was home to protect her. No one would dare to enter her house and violate her.

She sighed with a sense of relief.

She got off the bus and walked for a brief moment. The street was noticeably quiet.

No one was walking except her. She smiled. She put the key in the front door and turned it. She opened it and closed it behind her.

She put her head against the cold door frame. She was so pleased to be home.

She was no longer in danger. She was safe now as she turned the key.

Lucy was wrong about being safe. Someone was bashing the doorframe violently. She put her hand in front of her mouth in terror. The maniac pulled up the letterbox and pushed the knife inside. The knife was looking for her. It only found the letterbox and not being satisfied, attacked the doorframe.

Lucy shouted, "Help, Steve." Her voice echoed in the empty house. She forgot.

Steve was on holiday and he would not be back until the following day. She was alone and frightened like a child.

A neighbour's dog was barking, awakened by the noise.

Lucy ran up the bare wooden stairs but slipped, injuring her knee.

The maniac left the front door and smashed the back door. Lucy was trying to crawl forward with difficulty. Her knee was severely injured. She looked at the maniac. "I know you."

Those were the last words she said. The maniac stabbed her several times leaving her body lifeless and in a pool of blood. He started to cut her beautiful red dress.

He sexually touched her cold body. In his sick state of mind, he was enjoying himself.

Then he stopped. He heard the police sirens. There were a lot of people surrounding the house. He stood uprooted to the spot, knowing there was no escape.

Two officers entered the house by the back door and jumped on the maniac, disarming, and handcuffing him.

"Inspector, it is all clear."

"Well done officers! We have captured the maniac who has frightened the city for so long."

"You! I cannot believe it's you! You are the best officer in the force. You have arrested so many criminals and the public love you."

"Why, Constable George Brown, have you killed all these women?" The inspector looked with eyes so intense they seemed to be on fire.

"I don't know sir. I have this animal instinct in me. I did not know what I was doing."

"Take him away. Away from me."

The two officers took George Brown to the police car.

"Why would such a great officer do this? Look at this beautiful woman. She didn't deserve to die." The Inspector looked at her, his eyes full of tears, and covered her cold body with a blanket.

The Death Trap

A ndrew knew since his childhood what he would become as a
grown-up. He was a determined boy who would have his mind
made up. Despite the many difficulties and problems, he would face,
he would carry out his dream and no one or nothing would ever stop
him.

No one knew exactly what Andrew would become as he never told
anyone, not even his family, his big brother, or closest best friends. He
was not shy or ashamed at all. He hated people laughing at him for his
choices or talking behind his back. His family, big brother, and closest
best friends were worst of all, as they would interrogate and discourage
him if they knew his dream.

That is why he kept it a secret.

His family eventually would ask him about his future. Of all his
family, his dad was keenest to ask.

"Andrew, my son, what would you like to become as a grown-up?"

It was very difficult for little Andrew not to tell his dad. He wanted to
tell the entire world his dream. It was on the tip of his tongue and he
wanted to scream, but he was so used to keeping the secret he would
answer back, "I am not sure dad. I have so many dreams I have not
decided yet what I will do."

It did not help at all to keep the secret. His family thought Andrew was
an indecisive child who would not accomplish anything in life.

They were wrong.

He was obsessed with his dream. He would do anything for it.

"Dad, I have decided I do not want any presents for Christmas or my
birthday."

"Why so?" His dad stared at him, puzzled. "Let me check if you have a temperature." He put his hand on Andrew's forehead. Andrew's forehead was as cold as ice, but his eyes were so sparkling as if they were saying, "I mean it Dad. Just do it."

"Dad just give me pocket money instead."

"OK, son, if you are happy."

"I am Dad. Trust me."

Andrew saved all the money he received. Not one of the kids or adults would know where Andrew would spend it. He would do it secretly.

At the age of 10, he read an ad in the local paper shop. They were looking for a paperboy. He applied and got the job. He delivered the papers before school and after. The wage was not great, £2.00 an hour, Mondays to Saturdays. Despite the weather, it was raining almost every day, Andrew was not complaining at all.

He was very excited. "One step closer to fulfilling my dream," he repeated to himself.

One day, Peter saw Andrew carrying heavy bags and strange metallic parts.

Peter was Andrew's best friend and classmate. They had known each other since they were two years old. They had played together in the playground as Batman and Robin and as cowboys.

They confided in each other. There had never been secrets between them as they always told each other everything: which girl and sport they liked. They talked about everything until one day… Peter asked Andrew, "What will you do as a grown-up?"

Andrew looked at Peter with a sad face. Andrew liked Peter very much.

He considered him to be the twin brother he never had. He could not tell him about his dream. He never said one word.

Since then Andrew's attitude changed drastically. He and Peter never talked to each other as they did before. They avoided each other although they were in the same classroom. It seemed like they were complete strangers.

"Do you need any help, Andrew?"

"No thanks," Andrew replied very crossly. He was afraid that if Peter could see everything in the bag, he would tell everyone, and the entire village would know.

The village was full of nosy and eavesdropping neighbours who enjoyed talking behind people's backs.

Peter did not like Andrew's behaviour. He found it very irritating and annoying.

He hoped with time that Andrew would change for the better, so they could become friends again. Peter did not understand why Andrew had changed and he thought it was his fault. After turning it over in his mind for a long time, he believed it wasn't. "I did not do anything wrong." He was so upset, walking home with his head drooping between his shoulders.

Andrew felt sorry seeing Peter in this way, but he could not do anything about it.

He looked left and right, behind and in front of him, making sure nobody was following him. No one was. Walking slowly because of the heavy bags, Andrew took a rocky path which led to a green hill. It was a remote area where it was extremely dangerous and beautiful. The hill was cursed which is why it was dangerous.

The village named the hill 'The Death Trap' because if anyone went there, they would die in a fatal accident. That is, except for Andrew. He had been walking on The Death Trap for the past two years and he had always come back without a scratch.

Andrew loved The Death Trap. There was so much peace. It was so beautiful.

Andrew could relax under the old oak tree, hearing birds singing and smelling the fragrance of the flowers. He was even gladder there was nobody else who could reveal his dream.

All the books and strange metallic parts Andrew bought were in the old rotten shed on top of The Death Trap. They were hidden very well so even if anyone entered the shed, they would not find them easily.

He spent all his spare time after school and at the weekend in the shed until the sun was setting. His family was not worried about all the hours Andrew was spending outside. They probably thought he was playing with his classmates or best friend. They did not know that Andrew had fallen out with Peter.

For the sake of appearances, Peter behaved as if nothing had really happened between them. Peter covered up a lot of the times when Andrew could not explain where he had been, saying to his family, "Andrew has spent all afternoon with me playing in my garden," even though that was a lie.

Andrew was actually inside the shed on The Death Trap.

Later that day in his room, Andrew whispered to Peter: "Thanks for today. Please do not ask me where I have been," and Peter would not do that and find out anything.

Three years passed; Andrew had been moved to a different class with talented classmates. He did not feel displaced. He had learned a lot from the books he bought. He usually knew more than the old teachers. He had been feeling very uncomfortable in the old classroom. The kids used to laugh at him for his knowledge and intelligence. He felt like a fish out of water. It is bad being the best in the class

Being relocated to a new class was wonderful because he could talk to the other kids, who had the same intelligence and knowledge as him. Andrew did not feel alien now. Even the new teacher respected him very much. The old teachers were so horrible to Andrew. They were jealous of me. I know more than them Andrew was learning more complicated math mechanics, physics, and astronomy.

Other school hours were dedicated to physical and mental sports. Andrew loved everything more than before. His favourite hour was the chess club. He had never played chess before. He thought it was a boring game. The new teacher explained, "Chess is a fantastic game of strategy, brain and learning power.

46

You will not enjoy it at first, but the more you play, Andrew, the more your intelligence will grow with your capacity for learning and self-improvement."

"Yes, Sir."

The years went by. Life was becoming more difficult for Andrew. Apart from his part-time job and time spent in the shed on The Death Trap, his family wanted and demanded more time to be spent as a family.

Andrew had no choice but to tell lies to his family to keep his dream alive. He did not consider them to be lies but out-of-proportion excuses.

He remembered the time when he told his family about Thomas, an invisible friend, who had lost his mother. Thomas needed a mate to talk to and Andrew was there by his side. Andrew had to spend all afternoon cheering him up.

Thomas wept all the time. He could not understand why his mum was dead.

"She was so young. Why has God taken my mum away?"

"Aw. I know Thomas. I am sure your mum is watching over you. You have to be strong, so she can be proud of you!"

His family believed him completely. They were easily deceived or maybe they believed him because Andrew was particularly good at lying. It was the way he told the excuses, playing with their emotions, and making up plausible reality.

Even though Andrew had a vivid imagination, it was becoming ridiculously hard to come up with new excuses. He even recycled some of them after some time otherwise his family would start to be suspicious.

Andrew was so lucky that his family could 'drink' excuses like water and they had a poor memory.

This was playing in his favour. Anyway, his dream was getting closer and closer to being fulfilled.

He was incredibly careful not to be caught at night. When everyone was asleep, he got up in the middle of the night and went to the shed.

His family and big brother did not wake up as they slept very deeply. Most nights Andrew could not sleep anyway. They were snoring too loudly all night.

He had tried to make them stop, but nothing had worked.

Andrew was not upset with them. On the contrary, he was very thankful. He was able to make great progress towards his dream. At the same time, he avoided questions and found excuses.

Despite working at night, his school and work hours were not affected by the sleepless hours.

His adrenaline was keeping him very active. He never overslept or was late for school.

Andrew knew his life was changing for the better. It was a question of sooner rather than later.

Andrew could not believe the years were flying by so quickly. He did not care at all. He was excited. Eight years ago, when he had started his dream, he thought he would never succeed in finishing his creation. Now he only had to make a few adjustments and it would be ready for testing. He did not know if it would work.

Theory is one thing, practice is another.

It was coming up to his sixteenth birthday. Everybody was so excited, but Andrew wasn't. He didn't bother. Who cares, I won't be here. They don't care about my birthday. They behave as though they are pretending, I am very important. It's the same every year. They remember me on my birthday. What about the other 364 days in the year? Where were they?

His family was preparing a huge buffet for Andrew's friends and relatives.

They paid a magician and a DJ for the party. Who will turn up to my party? They don't know I don't have any friends. They will be very surprised when no one turns up!

48

Andrew had other worries on his mind. He needed to find other excuses so he could escape from this imprisonment. His family was tormenting him with many questions about the party.

Andrew was not coping very well. If he did not go out soon, he would blow up like a volcano, doing something silly and regretting it for the rest of his life.

"Sorry mum, I have to go out or I will explode."

"Andrew what about the balloons? What about the cake?"

"Mum, what about them? You decide. I am happy with anything."

"Andrew don't say that. Come on, help me. It's your birthday."

"It's still six weeks away. We've got time."

"I don't like rushing things. I am a perfectionist. I like organizing everything, so everything will go smoothly on your birthday."

"Thanks Mum. I have to go now. We will talk later."

"Always later Andrew. That's why you are undecided."

Andrew slammed the front door without saying one word back.

I hate my mum when she behaves like that. She is such a perfectionist. I cannot live this life any longer. Soon I will be out of here. Life is full of surprises. You cannot make plans. Something will come up and your plans will be out of the window.

The only place Andrew was happy was in the shed. Seeing his creation made him smile. His face lit up with joy.

In six weeks, I will test my creation. I hope there are no hiccups, and everything will work. It should be OK! Fingers crossed.

* * *

Six weeks were not long to wait. It is like saying 'piece of cake'.

Andrew's birthday also coincided with the prom at the school. It was a very chaotic day. While he was at school, his family was making the final arrangements for his party.

Andrew was not himself. His thoughts were miles away. He was arranging his day completely opposite from his family's plans.

The last thought was his birthday. He was preoccupied with his creation. There were some risks involved that he had never considered before. He was not scared.

It was normal to have doubts on the crucial day, which could change Andrew's life forever. He had to be strong and faithful. Everything would be fine.

I have worked so hard to achieve my creation and it would be silly to walk away now.

With this reinvigorated faith in himself, Andrew heard a shout.

"Andrew are you here with us?"

It was the math teacher. He had behaved very badly since his wife left him for a millionaire. He used to be a very understanding person who loved his students and helped the community. Since his wife went, the math teacher kept losing his temper without any reason.

I think he is still angry that his wife left him in this way. She was always so faithful and a loving wife until her mother died. Nobody knows why she left.

Some of the nosy neighbours heard she was complaining that her husband was too poor.

"Sorry, Sir. I could not understand this exercise."

"That is odd, Andrew. You have been the best in my class for years and you can't understand this simple exercise? Are you in love, Andrew?"

"No, Sir. My family has been stressing me out about my birthday for the past six weeks."

"I see."

"John, please explain this exercise to Andrew."

"Yes, Sir. Andrew, it is simple. A-B in brackets multiplied by CV/43R."

Andrew was not listening. His thoughts were in the shed on The Death Trap with his creation.

After that hiccup, Andrew had a better day. He did not have anyone tormenting him all day long.

After school, his family welcomed him with balloons and wished him Happy Birthday as soon he entered the front door.

Andrew was quite surprised some of his friends were there. They were dancing and giving him presents. He smiled at them, but his smile was false. He could not understand why they had turned up. In previous years they never came to my birthday. Maybe they had shown up for the food or the magician and DJ. I don't blame them. We have a massive garden where you could invite your relatives and friends for your wedding banquet.

Andrew did not remember anything about his birthday. He did not listen to the magician or the DJ's music. It seemed they were talking very slowly and from another world.

The day ended. Andrew received a kiss from a girl he had never met and 10 presents. He had a slice of his favourite lemon cake covered with whipped cream.

It did not taste great. It hadn't gone bad. It had lost his flavour. It seemed to be in a black-and-white movie where you don't have a sense of smell, taste, or hearing.

Andrew was getting ready for the school prom. He was in the bathroom making the final touches. A little bit of gel on his black, curly hair made him very cool.

He never bothered about his appearance. He just pretended to his family he was going out and he would have great fun.

Andrew was wearing a black jacket, trousers, and shoes. Underneath his jacket, he was wearing a posh shirt with long sleeves and a black bow tie.

"Andrew, it's late. Come on. Hurry up. It is half-past seven," his mother was shouting from downstairs. Your friends are here, waiting for you!"

"I'll be there in a sec," Andrew replied.

What is the rush? Nobody will notice me tonight. As soon I go to the prom and everyone has seen me, I will go to the shed.

Andrew walked down the stairs slowly. One step after another sounded like a long goodbye. At the bottom of the stairs, he looked back for a long minute trying to remember all the best memories he had had in the house and his room.

"Andrew, there you are. You look so good I'm sure you will break a lot of hearts tonight."

"Mum, you are embarrassing me. Stop it."

All his family was in the living room. His big brother was smiling at him. He was proud of him. His name was Stephen. He was 10 years older than Andrew and was getting married next month. May was getting warmer every single day.

Stephen had met his fiancée at the same school that Andrew attended. Stephen had never left her. They were soul mates. Her name was Jennifer. She was exceptionally beautiful, with long curly blonde hair and an amazing smile. "If you felt sad, her smile would make you smile too." She had a very curvy figure. *I am not surprised my brother is getting married. I would do the same if I were in his place.*

Stephen was hoping his brother would be lucky too. They had never argued in 10 years. They always got on very well. But Andrew had a secret plan for his future.

He never revealed it to a soul.

His mum and dad were proud of him for other reasons. They could see him growing into an adult despite their reservations of him as a person. They still believed Andrew was not ready for relationship commitment and responsibilities because of a lack of maturity.

Andrew was mature and wanted to prove it. He was waiting for the right moment.

He looked at his mum and dad for the last time and winked at them.

Despite the bad times we have had, I still loved you. Please remember me.

Please don't cry for me. I'll be OK. I'll always look down where I'll be! Andrew was thinking loudly.

"Go Andrew! Your friends are still outside!" his dad shouted.

"I'm going."

Andrew rushed out of the door. His friends were waiting, and they were very cross. They had been waiting for at least half an hour.

"Sorry guys! My mum is a pest. She would not let me leave. She gave me a lot of final recommendations for the prom."

"OK Andrew. Get in! We still have to pick up the girls," Peter answered back.

In the car, Joseph was sitting at the back. Who is this guy? I don't know him. *Maybe a friend of Peter's?*

"I'm sorry Andrew. Joseph, this is Andrew, my best and oldest friend. Andrew, this is Joseph, my brother."

"Nice to meet you, Joseph."

"Nice to meet you, Andrew."

They shook hands firmly.

"Which girls do we have to pick up tonight?"

"Steph and Lorraine," Peter replied.

Nice girls. Rumours were spreading I fancied them both. Of course, that was a lie. I did not have any feelings for anyone. My passion was my creation.

They were cheerleaders of the 'Lyons' American football team. They were exceptionally beautiful girls with blonde hair and green eyes and slim figures.

Everyone fancied them, but they were not keen on boys. They enjoyed their own company.

Some were saying they were lesbians. That was a rumour that had never been proved true.

They were wearing white dresses with matching shoes and bags. Their hair was in ponytails to the disappointment of the guys, except for Andrew.

"Guys, if you are going to ask about the lesbian rumour, we are not joining you.

We'll ask Steph's dad to take us to the prom."

"Don't worry girls. We won't. We are gents."

"OK, guys?"

"Yes, Peter."

"OK, Peter."

"Thanks guys. It has been an incredibly stressful week for us. Everyone was talking at school and no one gave us any peace."

During the journey, no one spoke. The guys were afraid to talk in case they brought up the subject or said something silly. Steph and Lorraine were too shy and were not talkative girls.

Andrew enjoyed the silence.

They arrived at the car park and a crowd surrounded the car at the sight of Steph and Lorraine.

The crowd followed Steph, Lorraine, Andrew, Peter, and Joseph inside the prom.

They wanted to find out if the rumours were true. Peter and Joseph were enjoying this short moment of fame. Steph and Lorraine started dancing straight away.

The music was very groovy. The DJ was playing the latest pop songs.

Andrew smiled. His chance came unexpectedly. Nobody would notice his early departure from the prom as all the attention was concentrated on Steph, Lorraine, Peter, and Joseph.

Andrew walked out of the back door.

He was so excited. The time had come to test his creation. He skipped along the rocky path leading to the shed on The Death Trap. *I cannot believe I will test my creation tonight. Not one of my family, best friends or police will find me!*

Tonight, my life will change forever. I will not come back. I will be gone.

There were no doubts in Andrew's mind. He knew what he was doing. He opened the door of the shed. He went inside his creation. With his fingers crossed, just a sign of good luck, Andrew turned on the light and the engine. The engine made a very low hum. His creation was a very metallic composition in the shape of a saucer. Andrew was overjoyed. So far, his creation was responding. So far, my creation is working well. Let's see what happens when I move the controls.

Andrew moved the controls of the spaceship. It went forward and upward in a fraction of a second, breaking the speed of sound. Andrew had a quick look down, a last goodbye to his planet earth. He was not sad, nor did he regret his choice. He was delighted.

He was in space. "Other planets and galaxies to explore. I can't wait. Let's see how fast my creation can go," he said, moving the controls further.

The spaceship went into hyperspace and disappeared into the billion lights of the universe.

Peter and Joseph had a fantastic time at the prom.

They danced and got drunk. They were so drunk, Mr. Brown, their teacher, had to take them home.

"Peter, what a night. We have been so lucky. Anne kissed me and gave me her number."

"Yes, Peter, what a night. I was kissed by someone I didn't even know. Do you know where Andrew is?"

"Is he not with you, Joseph?"

"No. He is not with me. He was definitely with us at the prom. I don't know what happened to him. Mr. Brown, have you seen Andrew?"

"I've been looking for Andrew in the building, but he is not here. He probably went home early."

The next morning horrible news spread through the village. Andrew was missing, and the police were involved in searching for him. They were looking for him everywhere, even beyond a 50-mile radius. Andrew's family was devastated and confused. They could not believe their son had disappeared. They were looking in the wrong direction. They should have looked up. Andrew was somewhere else. Only he would know where he was, but for the first time, he was enjoying every minute of his life. Nobody would be tormenting him, and he would learn more of the universe. Andrew would never come back and learn what the future had in store for his family. He just wanted to fulfil his dream: flying in the universe. He had done so. He was so proud of himself. During his exploration, he recorded all his knowledge and experience on his computer as a testimonial of his life's achievement.

Lucas and Doris

L ucas was woken up by the sunlight of the new day. Unaware of the future events ahead, he was feeling incredibly happy. Doris's perfume, an intense lily fragrance, scented the bedroom.

Her dressing gown was lying on the bed. Lucas picked it up and smelt her. He closed his eyes. She was there.

The passionate and intense love that had happened the night before had changed Lucas's life forever. He had been single for a long time, but now he had found his soul mate.

He looked around. Doris was not in the bedroom. "Doris, where are you?"

Lucas shouted.

His voice echoed around the million-pound yacht, but there was no response.

Lucas looked at the clock. It was midday.

He became increasingly worried and concerned.

Doris should be home by now, but she wasn't. Where was she? Did something happen to her? She never stayed out so long.

Many questions and thoughts overcrowded his mind.

A terrible feeling came over Lucas. Doris was in danger and he was the only person who could save her.

With no time to spare, he got dressed and started to look for her.

He knew Doris was going shopping.

She told me last night before I fell asleep.

Despite searching in every grocery shop and supermarket, none of the staff remembered seeing Doris that morning.

It was a small town on a small island. I am sure someone must have seen Doris.

She was five-foot-six-inches tall with blue eyes and blonde hair. She had a slim figure and was wearing a pink dress and shoes. No one seemed to have seen a woman with this description.

Maybe she forgot about going shopping and she went to visit Carlos?

This thought gave Lucas's spirit and morale a boost. He convinced himself that was what she had done.

We all met up and laughed about her imaginary disappearance.

Carlos was a friend of long-standing.

He had a villa with a swimming pool overlooking the sea.

Although Carlos hated living there, he loved being at the seaside for health reasons.

Carlos suffered from asthma and the sea air made him feel better. "It is the fresh and clean environment you need," the doctor had recommended.

"Hi, Carlos. How are you?"

"Hi, Lucas. I'm fine thank you. How are you?"

"I'm worried and upset."

"Why, Lucas?"

"I am looking for Doris, but I cannot find her anywhere. I went to the supermarkets and grocery shops, but no one had seen her. Have you?"

"No. Last time I saw her was last night. Maybe you could try her favourite café.

She might have met an old friend and gone for a drink."

"Thank you, Carlos. You have been a great help."

"You are welcome Lucas."

Again, Lucas set about searching for Doris, but he was getting more upset and frustrated. In all the cafés and bars the same answer emerged. No one had seen a woman of that description.

It was possible she had passed unnoticed or it could be that something terrible had happened to her. It seemed to Lucas that the second possibility was the more realistic.

Then an idea came into his head. "Of course," Lucas shouted, slapping his forehead which was cold with sweat.

Some passers-by stared at him, thinking he had lost the plot.

She might have felt ill and been taken to the hospital.

From the pocket of his jacket, he took out his mobile phone.

"Come on Doris… come on Doris be there…" Lucas was thinking, nervously pressing the buttons of his mobile phone.

His worries seemed to fade momentarily, and a new hope arose.

Again, the bad news prevailed. No woman of her description had been taken to the hospital.

At least she is not ill or badly injured, but, where is she?

I do not know where to look. I have been searching everywhere and I cannot find her. She has simply vanished from the face of the earth!

After walking around for three hours, with tired legs, low morale, and a worried face, he found himself outside the police station. Another hope was shattered, with dismay he walked inside.

The police station was crawling with activity. The telephones were ringing continuously, but no one answered them.

The cops were too busy restraining two disruptive tattooed criminals who had been arrested for bank robbery.

The two convicts were swearing and resisting incarceration so four police officers had no choice but to drag them into the cells by force.

While this was happening, a constable was sipping his coffee, watching the scene, and the smell of the fresh coffee brought Lucas back to reality.

"Good afternoon, Constable Smith."

"Good afternoon, Sir."

"My name is Lucas Dominguez. I have been searching for my girlfriend Doris Rodriguez all afternoon, but I cannot find her anywhere."

"When did you last see your girlfriend?"

"Last night before I fell asleep."

"At the moment, Sir, it is too early to involve the police in this matter. We have a policy of waiting 24 hours for people who go missing. Not unless you know someone wants to harm her."

"Not as far as I know."

"Do not worry, Sir. I am sure she will come home soon. Probably she is home now and is wondering where you are."

"Thank you, Constable Smith."

"My duty, Sir."

Lucas walked home with renewed hope. He arrived and dreamt that Doris was running towards him hugging him and kissing him all over.

Constable Smith was wrong.

He walked into the kitchen and found a shopping list on the table.

To buy: eggs, potato scones, unsmoked bacon, and milk.

"Where is Doris?" The same question was going around and around in his head.

Doris was wondering the same. She woke up in a dark room, filthy and with a horrible smell.

A half-eaten rat was lying dead near her. The smell was horrendous and nauseous.

Other rats were ready to attack their friendly corpse, but they were afraid. They were staying at a safe distance.

Doris was not scared at all.

She was feeling great and disorientated at the same time.

How did I get here? Where am I?

In the corner of the room, the light of a new dawn was coming through a gap in the wall.

Doris was desperate to escape the mysterious and terrifying adversary. She knew her life was in danger.

She looked around to find a get-away.

Meanwhile, the light was slowly approaching her. A door nearby was opened.

In a flash, she flew through it.

The other room had the same horrendous and nauseous smell, but there was no gap in any wall. Doris felt safe.

She looked at herself in case she was hurt.

She noticed there was a stain on her pink dress. She touched it and she was shocked.

That's blood! How did it get there?

Where is Lucas? Last time I saw him was last night. I can't recall what happened after that.

The only thing I know is I can't go out. I don't know why I'm afraid. My instinct tells me my life is in danger. I will die if I do. I will wait until sunset.

Doris did not feel hungry or thirsty. She knelt on the floor all day long.

* * *

On the other side of the island, more frustrated and worried, Lucas had a brilliant idea, sitting and smoking his pipe in his rocking chair on the wooden deck.

He felt peaceful and had a serene smile on his face. The rocking chair reminded him of his childhood. In his early years, he had cried many times and his mum knew that rocking the cradle was the only way to make him smile.

After all the previous failures, it seemed this time he would succeed in finding Doris.

Lucas had a friend whose name was Jose Santiago. Jose was a private investigator and, over many years, had cracked very difficult cases that the police had not managed to solve.

His instinct and intelligence helped him on many occasions to see the entire crime while the police only had fragments of it.

In a powerful positive state of mind, Lucas dialled Jose's number.

"Good morning, Jose. It's Lucas speaking."

"Good morning, Lucas. How can I help you?"

"I have been searching everywhere for my girlfriend, Doris Rodriguez, all day and talked to anyone I know. I've even spoken to the police, but they could not help me. There is a 24-hours policy for missing people."

"That's right, Lucas. Hmm. That's weird. Can you tell me more about her?"

"Doris is five-foot-six-inches with blue eyes and blonde hair. She has a slim figure and is wearing a pink dress and shoes. She is 29 years old with a beauty spot on her neck."

"Thanks Lucas. Just a moment… I'm checking on my laptop. With this description, only one woman is coming up. Her name is Doris Rodriguez, but…"

The three minutes suspense was killing Lucas.

It seemed an eternity. "… She died 40 years ago."

"That's absurd. Doris is 29 years old. Something is not adding up. Jose, are you sure your laptop did not make a mistake?"

"My laptop has never failed in 20 years."

"I don't understand, Jose."

"I know Lucas. She might have lied to you about her full name."

"She might, but I'm pretty sure she told me the truth."

"In any case, if you wish I'll use all my resources to find her."

"Thanks Jose."

"It's my duty. My fee is £10,000, Lucas."

"That's fine."

"I'll call you with any news, Lucas. Goodbye."

"Goodbye, Jose."

Lucas was very confused. Jose was right. He had never been wrong in 20years.

Could Doris have lied to him? Or could Jose's laptop have not been updated with the latest information?

Lucas was certain Jose would eventually find Doris.

Despite his many doubts, Lucas was calm and relaxed sitting in his rocking chair waiting for Jose's phone call.

The day flew by at an incredible speed. Sunset was approaching. The shadows were becoming longer, and a cold breeze was blowing.

Doris did not move all day. She was still kneeling on the same spot. She felt happy. She knew the sun was disappearing below the horizon.

Darkness was winning the battle against the light, approaching in every direction.

The cold breeze turned sinister causing all the people of the island to shiver. It was so creepy to be outside no one dared walk in the streets.

For one-hundred years, word of mouth had taught people: "Never go out in a sinister breeze otherwise you will die."

The legend was 'creepy evil creatures would escape from their graves, walk and kill innocent people at night!'

No one could confirm if it was a true or imaginary story as nobody had dared walk in the streets and, if someone had done so, no one had come back alive to tell!

Doris Continued Her Quest Through The Sinister Breeze.

Meanwhile, Carlos was admiring the sea. He did not believe in the legend. He thought the legend was an imaginary story for frightening the children.

He was unaware of the danger.

Doris saw him, and, in a flash, she appeared behind him, surrounded by black clouds.

Doris whispered, "Hi Carlos," kissing him on the neck.

She stared at the new moon shining.

"Kill him, kill him," the voice whispered louder in her ear.

A powerful evil force invaded and possessed her.

Her teeth and nails turned longer and sharper.

Doris was ready to bite, but… a whistling sound flew through the air and something struck her back.

"Oh, dear." Those were her last words.

Her body turned to ashes.

Carlos turned his head around.

"Doris, where are you?"

Nobody replied.

The following day, Lucas was sitting on his rocking chair sipping a Bacardi and coke, still waiting for Jose's phone call.

An anonymous envelope arrived.

Lucas opened it and found a gold necklace with the inscription 'Love you always, Doris', a sharp wooden stake with some ashes, and a piece of paper.

'Doris will never come back. Please pay £10,000.'

Lucas cried for a few minutes. His tears rolled down his face and he dried them with his right hand.

He realized Doris had gone forever and he had to live without her.

So, he decided to leave these painful memories and sad island and cross the sea for the rest of his life. Nobody has ever seen Lucas again after he disappeared beyond the horizon.

Expect the Unexpected

M artin O'Brien was an ordinary man. His life was so ordinary that every day went the same way. Martin went to work on the bus and walked for 20 minutes to the office in the centre of Glasgow.

His job involved phoning people to arrange appointments for windows, doors, conservatories, and garage doors to be replaced.

The job was not great. Martin was continuously abused by people, who insulted him or slammed the phone down on him. His job was not a selling job, it was market research. The people getting the phone calls did not understand.

They were probably tired of getting phone calls when they were too busy or expecting an important call or were about to go out for work.

Martin was trying to explain to one person, "This is not a sales phone call. It is just market research."

"Do not care, go to hell."

Martin looked depressed and put the receiver down.

He needed the money so badly. His bank account was always overdrawn. The money was coming in very handy for paying his rent, travel, and food.

The company was paying him £4.50 an hour, which was illegal as the minimum wage was £5.52 an hour, but Martin did not have the courage to sue the company demanding an increase in his wages as he was scared he would lose his job.

Times were tough. There were not many jobs. Martin had been looking for a job for the past three months. He had used all his savings paying the rent, food, and utility bills. Miserably, the money had run out. Two weeks ago, Martin had taken the last paper on Monday morning which advertised jobs.

If I do not get another job soon, I don't know how I am going to pay the bills, Martin thought.

He did not have much choice. He made few phone calls; unfortunately, all the jobs had been taken except for one.

It was for market research. *I don't have anything to lose*, he thought.

"Good morning, my name is Martin O'Brien. I would like to apply for the market research vacancy advertised in the paper."

"Good Morning, Martin O'Brien. That's great. We have an interview slot tomorrow at 11:00 am. We are at 3, Bothwell Street in the centre of Glasgow. The dress code is smart."

"Thanks."

Martin was jumping with joy. I can't fail. They take anyone, even people who do not have any experience.

The next morning Martin arrived half an hour early for the interview. Despite being nervous, he got the job.

Martin came home, and he was feeling more enthusiastic about his life. At least I do not have to be worried anymore about money. I will have money to pay my rent, food, and travel and have some for me.

Martin lived alone in his flat. His family died many years ago. He had never had a girlfriend. Martin was a very average guy. He was not ugly or handsome.

He never had girls chasing him when he was younger.

I never cared about girls. I heard from my ex-friends all the troubles they had been through. Some of my friends married the wrong women who married their husbands for money or committed adultery after four weeks of marriage.

Martin did not have that trouble. He did not sleep with a woman for quite a while.

He was not a virgin. He had lost his virginity when he was 16 years old.

His Mum and Dad did not know when and where it happened.

Some weird letters were coming in the post. Martin did not recognize the senders.

They were all good news.

One sender apologized to Martin, saying he forgot to pay him last week and he would pay him by cheque next week.

Martin was puzzled. He scratched his head, and he did not understand.

I do not know who this guy is. I am sure it might be a mistake. He has confused me with somebody else.

The next week, a letter arrived with a cheque for £300, payable to Martin O'Brien, and he paid it into his bank account. Maybe it is my lucky week, Martin thought.

I do not care if this guy made a mistake. I have banked the cheque and if the right person demands this money, I will say I never got it.

Things turned weirder every day.

One day when he went to work, an old, big, short woman approached Martin.

She looked 51 years old and she was shaped like an apple.

"Martin, do you remember me? I'm Michelle."

"Sorry, have you confused me with somebody else?"

"No, it is you, Martin O'Brien. You made love to me last week in my apartment.

I just came to see you to warn you; my husband knows everything about us! He is furious like a cat! He wants to kill you! Be careful."

I truly do not know that woman. I definitely never made love to her. I do not care about her husband. Something weird is going on. Things are happening to me and I do not know why. I am not a man with a lot of sex appeal so that women chase me. I am not Richard Gere.

Martin shrugged his shoulders.

He went to work, and he had a normal day, being abused, and getting poor results.

Tomorrow will be better than today, Martin thought and hoped.

On the bus, a stunning lassie with long legs approached him and whispered in his ear: "Since last time I saw you I cannot live without you. I dream of you."

I do not know her, but I do not mind.

Martin did not care, and he was pleased. Something was happening to him.

Finally, after an ordinary life, things are changing for the better.

The lassie was called Jennifer. She was six-feet tall with long legs, a curvy figure, green eyes, and short hair.

Martin let Jennifer into his apartment and, without a minute to lose, they both took off their clothes and made love.

She must be taking drugs and sleeping around, and she confuses people.

Something came into Martin's head. Could it be possible somebody else looks like me, uses my name, and does all the things I have not done, pretending to be me? There could be a twin brother somewhere I did not know about, with the same face. My dad and mum never told me.

Certainly, I have to expect the unexpected.

Martin's life became fantastic. He got married and had two children. He never got divorced and he also found a well-paid job. Martin was very happy and thankful for everything that came into his life.

The Traveller

J oseph Loser was not a lucky person either in word and or in real life. Of his entire family, he was the only unlucky one. His sister Sarah had won the lottery and scooped £1,500,000. His oldest brother Mark was running an international company in Brazil and his wages were £100,000 a year.

His mum Samantha was helping her husband Martin in their restaurant in Monaco and the restaurant was a very lucrative business bringing in around£1,200,000 a year. They were both bringing home £250,000.

Joseph was unemployed and without a penny in his bank account. He was a loser.

He could not do anything right. He could not even get a girlfriend or keep a job for longer than a week.

I feel so hopeless and inept.

To make things even more depressing, all his friends were better than him.

They had great jobs, money in the bank, and stunning girlfriends or wives.

Joseph did not have anything at all.

I wish I had a bit of luck in my life. Just a bit. I do not want too much. I would like to have some money and a girlfriend, so my family and friends will get off of my back and stop laughing at me. It is so depressing and humiliating having these people treating me in this way.

I have done everything I can. I have applied for jobs, but I can't last longer than a week, and I can't get a girlfriend. I am a nice guy. I treat women as though they were princesses. Nowadays women like being treated badly and they think nice guys are boring, Joseph thought.

There is nothing wrong with me. I am six-feet tall. I have got blue eyes and brown hair. I only lack confidence. Apart from this, I am a good, honest, and handsome man.

Joseph's mobile phone was vibrating on the bed.

It was Patrick. Patrick was his very old friend from school. Patrick was very clever. He did not care about money or women. He was only interested in his inventions. He was obsessed. He spent all his time, energy, and money on them.

"Hi, Patrick, how are you doing?"

"Hi, Joseph. I am great thanks. I am so happy."

"Why is that, Patrick?"

"I have finally completed my invention."

"Really, Patrick? What is it this time?"

"I have finally completed my invention."

"Really, Patrick? What is it this time?"

"I can't tell you over the phone. Maybe someone is listening. We need to meet."

"Okay, tell me when."

Patrick was worried someone could steal his inventions and make money, but the worst part was that they would take all his credits. That is why Patrick secretly invited Joseph to his lab and only Joseph knew where it was.

Patrick trusted Joseph with all his heart, and he knew Joseph would never betray him.

Joseph wrote down the time, took his jacket, and went out.

He knocked on the door twice.

"Are you alone, Joseph?"

"Yes, I am."

"Did anyone follow you?"

"No, trust me. You are the only friend I have. I would never do anything to jeopardize our friendship, you know that."

"I know. I just wanted to make sure. These days I never trust anyone."

"I know, Patrick."

Patrick opened the door and Joseph closed it behind him.

"What is it this time?"

"This is an amazing invention that could change history forever."

"Wow! I am intrigued."

Patrick went to his secret room and came back with an object wrapped in a small blue silk blanket.

He unravelled it.

"Double wow," Joseph shouted and immediately covered his mouth with his hand in a way to say sorry for having shouted so that someone could have heard and come to see what it was.

The object was a screwdriver with a blue beam.

"This is not an ordinary screwdriver. This is a time-travel screwdriver. If you turn this knob up, you will go into the future and if you turn it down, you will go into the past."

"I understand, Patrick. Have you already travelled?"

"Yes, I have Joseph. The things I have seen. They are amazing."

"Just a moment, Patrick. What if you change the past and future? You will create a paradox."

"I know that and, don't worry, nothing has changed. Do you think I am that stupid?"

"I am sorry, Patrick."

"No problem, Joseph. I phoned you because I want to help you."

"What are you going to do, Patrick?"

"Everyone knows you are unlucky."

"Yes, sure. Thanks for rubbing in it Patrick."

"… and we are going to change that! I am going to send you into the past with a mission of betting on many sporting events where you already know the results, so you cannot lose."

"Right, Patrick. Good plan. I like that," Joseph's eyes started brightening up.

"I have here an almanac from 1970 to 2000. What you have to do is just bet some money on the winner in any sport you like but be careful not to bet more than twice in a betting shop otherwise they will get suspicious."

"OK. Thanks Patrick. I am a bit worried. Are you sure it will work?"

"Don't be a chicken now Joseph."

Patrick selected the date 12/04/1970 on the screwdriver and gave it to Joseph.

"Simply press this button and you will travel to this date. When you want to come back, just turn up the knob and select a date. OK, Joseph?"

Joseph closed his eyes pressing the button and a sucking force took him into the past. He disappeared into thin air.

"Good luck Joseph," said Patrick.

Joseph found himself in the past and with a stake of £10 he made £3,000,000in a week.

For Patrick, 50 seconds had passed when Joseph came back with the news.

Joseph appeared out of thin air.

"Hi Patrick. Look how much money I have."

"I know Joseph. You should have been more careful. You have brought so much attention to yourself."

"I am sorry Patrick. Next time I will be more careful. Yes, next time. I want to explore time and space."

"No, you won't."

Patrick ran towards Joseph to steal the screwdriver from him, but Joseph knew Patrick's intentions. "I won't give up the only thing that has changed my life forever." Joseph turned down the knob, selected a date, and disappeared into thin air.

Patrick never saw Joseph again. He read all his adventures in books and magazines. His name was known all over the world.

Certainly, Joseph Loser no longer lived up to his name. He was recognized as a man who could not fail, as failure was not acceptable.

Christopher and Simaco

C hristopher Matthews was born on Friday 13 April 1917. His family knew this son would not be different from them. He was born unlucky, like the rest of the family. It had started with the great-great-greatgrandfather in 1780 who lost all his fortune in a gambling business. Since then, all the males in the following generations had tried to turn the misfortune around with very risky gambles.

All their attempts failed miserably. "This curse will never break up. It will carry on forever and ever throughout the generations," Sebastian commented loudly to the family. He, too, had failed in his life. He had a great idea for making money.

His idea was very well thought through with a sound financial basis, limiting his costs to the minimum so he could make a large profit.

However, Sebastian knew the curse would find a way to strike his business. He hoped this time would be different. He would break the curse.

Sebastian had a friend called Frank. Frank was selling him imported gems from South Africa. They were very cheap as no one knew about these new precious stones, but as soon as demand increased, there was more competition causing the price to fall, thereby reducing Sebastian's market.

Sebastian foolishly reduced his prices too. That was the last straw for his great business. With high losses, he had no choice but to borrow money. He borrowed like there was no tomorrow. His debts eventually caught up with him.

They spiralled higher and higher until he had to sell his house. Now he lived with his wife, Clara, a twelve-year-old daughter, Sarah, and his new baby boy, Christopher, under the Healthy Bridge in a carton box. They did not feel cold or miserable. They were very adaptable in these new circumstances. It was very weird. The Healthy Bridge brought Sebastian a lot of money when he was selling the South African gems and now it was his poor home.

Sebastian did not forget what his grandfather and father had told him before they died. "Son, whatever you do, the curse cannot be broken. We have tried and failed. The more you try to be rich, the more you will become poor. The best way will be to just leave it. Enjoy what you have and do not ask for more."

It was not that simple. It was an obsession for the Matthews. If Sebastian broke the curse, good luck would run through future generations, on and on. He had lost his chance. He knew he had no way to get his fortune back.

When the curse strikes you, no matter what you do, it will not let you get back your feet again. My only hope is my son, Christopher. He was born on a bad day and year. We have no chance, Sebastian was thinking. Despite the poor conditions, the Matthews would not give up. They made the best of what they had. No one in the community helped them with clothes, food, or a place to live.

They were completely alienated. They couldn't understand why. Christopher did not miss either toys or sweets. He had gorgeous vivid blue eyes. Clara had never seen such gorgeous eyes in her entire life.

The oddest thing about Christopher was not his eyes, but his hair. It was ginger.

In the entire Matthews's history, no male or female child had ever had ginger hair. It was very peculiar.

"Do you find the colour of Christopher's hair very strange, darling?"

"Yes, my dear. I have never seen anyone in my life with ginger hair, certainly no one in our family.

"Christopher's hair is unique and rare. Could it be a good sign?"

Certainly, it was not a good sign for Christopher since everyone teased him about it.

"Look at the ginger boy!" or "Come on ginger!"

They were upsetting Christopher and he was getting angrier and angrier. There were occasions when Christopher lost control and pushed people down the street or turned the café tables upside down. Some of the passers-by had no choice but to call the police to the scene. Christopher would run off before they arrived. He was not a bad boy. He was just tired that his life was so difficult. He wanted to be someone very important, so people would respect him. He was fed up.

"Christopher, stop moaning."

"Mum, I'm fed up living here. Can't we have house, food, and clothes like everyone else?"

"Son! Be grateful! We've got each other and that counts more than anything else.

Our love is bigger than material possessions."

"I know dad, but… you don't have people laughing at you for your ginger hair."

"People envy you because you are different."

"No, I'm not different! I'm a beggar."

Sebastian's face turned red with anger. "Christopher, go away and only come back with an apology for your cheekiness!"

Christopher was feeling sorry for his cheeky words. He did not mean them. He did not want to see his family in this situation. He wanted to help, but he did not know how. His dad told him about the curse. It is all in vain. How can I help my dad if I am unlucky like the rest of my family?

As he was walking down the street, Christopher saw something shining between the paving stones. It was a silver coin. Christopher picked it up. It was a shilling.

It's a brand-new shilling. It was so shiny. He felt a strange vibration in his hand and looked at the metallic reflection. *My dad will be proud of me for this small fortune.*

"No, do not spend me. Please keep me."

Christopher looked around. There was nobody else except him and the coin.

"Is there anyone behind that tree?" No one replied. Again, the voice spoke. "I'm here in your hand. I am a lucky coin. You make a wish, and I will grant it."

Christopher was very confused. Was it possible a silver magic coin could exist?

Could it be a fruit of his imagination? His stomach was rumbling.

Christopher hadn't eaten a proper meal for a long time. *That's right! I am starving, and I hear things!*

"I know what you are thinking. I am a magic coin, and I can speak."

"If you are real, how is that?"

"I used to be a genie in a bottle and an evil witch transformed me into a silver coin. I defeated her, but for revenge, she put a spell on me!"

"I see. What is your name, silver coin?"

"Simaco."

"Nice to meet you, Simaco. My name is Christopher Matthews."

"Nice to meet you, Christopher. You are a mess. Christopher."

"I know, Simaco. My family is very poor, and we live under the Healthy Bridge."

"Christopher, have you always been poor?"

"No, Simaco. My dad used to have house, food, and clothes, but we lost everything because we are unlucky. We have been under a curse since 1780.

The curse can only be broken by a male of the family and our misfortune can be turned around. The thing is... I don't know how."

"I know how, Christopher. Destiny brought me here today."

"That's right! I will take you to my dad."

Christopher was running around the people in the street. His feet were burning hot and he was feeling wobbly. I am feeling sick, but I need to speak to my dad.

Simaco is the only way to break the curse. Christopher knew that he was running out of breath.

"Sorry… Dad," he said in a husky voice. "I am so sorry."

Christopher was catching his breath.

"I accept your apologies."

"Dad, I have great news. I had found a shiny shilling in the street."

"That's great, Son."

"This is a magic shilling."

"Magic shillings don't exist. I don't want to hear it. This is the last time you tell me stories."

"OK, Dad," Christopher replied, lowering his head with a sad face.

"Darling, you have been too harsh on Christopher!"

"My dear, I haven't. I don't want people to think Christopher is demented."

Christopher did not blame his dad. He had told so many imaginary stories that his father could not take them anymore.

It is a shame my dad didn't let me explain. He would understand. "Why didn't you speak up, Simaco? You could have helped me out!"

"Sorry Christopher, the only person who can hear me is you! The adults don't believe in genies or witches!"

"So, what now? Christopher, have you forgotten? I can grant wishes. Just rub me and make a wish."

"How many wishes?"

"Three."

"I need to think. I have only three wishes. I cannot waste them."

"Don't worry, Christopher. Take your time. Don't rush straight away."

"Thanks, Simaco."

"You're welcome, Christopher."

Christopher was in a very sticky situation. He did not know where to turn.

Should I choose to be selfish by making myself rich or try to help others? After much thought, Christopher decided.

"Simaco, I've decided."

"Please tell me more, Christopher."

"I want to be rich. I want to be important, so people will respect me."

"Are you sure, Christopher?"

"Yes, I am Simaco. I can always do good."

"Yes, you can. So, what is your first wish, Christopher?"

"I wish… to be the richest boy in the entire world."

Christopher closed his eyes as tight as he could. It was a strange feeling. It seemed like waiting for a present you know is coming to be wrapped up.

Christopher was so excited. He could not wait any longer.

"All done, Christopher."

He opened his eyes slowly. He looked around, but nothing had changed. He was on the same spot wearing the same old torn clothes with bare feet and muddy face, arms, and legs. Christopher looked at Simaco with angry eyes and face.

"Simaco, you have disappointed me! You said you can grant my wishes.

I'm still the same poor boy. You're a fake."

"I'm not a fake. Be patient, Christopher."

"Why should I keep you?"

"Christopher, wait until the morning…"

"OK, I will. If you fail me tomorrow, I will throw you into the river. Is it a deal?"

"Done deal, Christopher."

* * *

Sebastian came back with some bread, beans, and fruit. He lit the fire and cooked the beans inside a rotten pan. His face and hands were muddy. He had lost a lot of weight like all his family since they had become poor. He had a hacking cough.

It was getting worse every single day.

I think my dad will die very soon if nothing happens out of the ordinary.

Sebastian had begged in all types of weather: fog, heavy rain, burning sun, freezing cold and blistering snow.

He was desperate. He would do anything to keep his family fed. Sebastian could only just survive on the money they had.

With years going by, life was becoming very tough for everyone and the passersby dropped fewer coins in Sebastian's torn and worn hat just to eat beans, some fruit, and bread.

Water was in abundance as they were living near a river. The river was drinkable.

They used it to wash themselves. They enjoyed it when it was a hot summer's day. They just jumped in to keep themselves cool. The problem was they had to share it with everyone else. They did not mind. The Matthews were very understanding and easy-going people.

"I hope Simaco doesn't let me down tomorrow. If I am the richest boy in the world, we won't have to live like this anymore."

"Christopher, where have you put the shilling you found?"

"Sorry dad, I think I lost it," Christopher replied, keeping the coin in his right fist behind his back.

Christopher didn't like telling lies to his dad. He had no other choice. Simaco was becoming a very valuable friend.

I cannot give Simaco away. Apparently, Simaco said it can grant wishes. If it doesn't, I can always give it to my dad tomorrow morning.

"Christopher, never mind."

Christopher was still starving after dinner. He could not get any more food.

The night brought a very bad storm. Christopher was so tired he didn't hear the thunder and the heavy rain falling. He fell asleep and was only woken up by the sun of the new day. Something felt weird. He could smell flowers. Where is this fragrance coming from? he thought.

There were no flowers growing near the bridge. It was all cement-based. There was grass, but that was at least a couple of miles away.

Christopher's eyes were not completely open. The image was very blurred. He was half-asleep and half-awake.

He scratched his head. He couldn't understand where he was. Then he rubbed his eyes in disbelief.

The lilies were inside a glass vase on a bedside cabinet.

Christopher had slept on a comfortable goose-down mattress and pillow. The bed was made of wood and the bed linen was French, made of wool with a drawing of a swan and a lake in the middle. Christopher pinched his face.

There was a man at the far end of the room, and he was drawing the curtains with an identical pattern.

The room was so enormous Christopher could imagine himself dancing. The ceiling had an angel pattern.

Wow, what a beautiful room! Christopher threw back his bedclothes and he was amazed. He was spotless. He had never seen his skin so pink before. He was wearing new cotton pyjamas.

"Good morning, Sir," the man said after finishing drawing the curtains.

"Good morning."

"Would you like to have breakfast in bed, Sir?"

"Yes, sure," Christopher was feeling amazingly comfortable even though he didn't know where he was.

He got out of bed and followed the man, whose name was Jimmy, and was, apparently, to be his personal servant.

His bedroom was situated on the south side of the house, as it was warmer, and it was bigger than any other room.

Christopher stopped for a moment to look at all the paintings, statues, and suits of armour in the long corridor. He had never seen so many beautiful objects in his life. His dad had mentioned them to him. He had always listened carefully, imagining what it would be like if he could be rich.

Christopher touched them making sure they were real. I'm not dreaming. They are solid and cold.

On the side of the corridor wall, Christopher admired a decorated glass. I don't have time to waste. The man is walking down the stairs. The staircase was made of mahogany, with a handrail and white marble angel half-boost balusters, covered by a red carpet. Christopher was so excited. He ran down the stairs missing some of them as he jumped two at a time.

At the bottom of the stairs, Christopher found a mosaic floor, the large wooden front door, and a long corridor leading to the kitchen, study, dining room, and garden.

It would take me ages to explore all this house. I hope I am not sleeping.

Please don't be a dream, be real!

"Good morning, Christopher. Yes, it's all real."

"How Simaco?"

"That is my power to grant wishes."

"So, I'm not dreaming? It won't disappear. It will be here forever?"

"Not unless…"

"Please, not unless what, Simaco?"

"If you wish it not to be here, it will vanish, Christopher."

"No, I won't, Simaco. Can I lose it though?"

"What do you mean, Christopher?"

"I mean like my dad when he lost everything?"

"Anyone can lose everything. You are in control of your life. It's up to you what you do."

Christopher was delighted. His dad would be proud of him.

"My dad will be so happy. I have succeeded in defeating the curse and have become rich."

Christopher remembered something. The curse cannot be defeated. It will come back and take everything I own.

Unless... I wish for it.

"Simaco, I have decided to make another wish."

"Are you sure, Christopher? Remember there are only two wishes remaining."

"I know, Simaco. I wish I have luck."

"All done. Your wish had been granted."

"Great! Let's go and see what happens!"

Christopher could not wait for the result. "If I succeed, I will have broken the curse."

"Hello, Sir."

"Hello."

"My name is Jimmy, your personal servant."

"Hello, Jimmy."

"I see you have decided to come down for your breakfast, Sir."

"Yes, Jimmy. But before I have my breakfast, I would like to ask you if you could place a bet for me."

"A bet, Sir? It is too risky. You have money. You don't need to bet."

"Jimmy, please help me."

"Certainly, Sir. I'll bring the newspaper."

"Thanks, Jimmy."

Jimmy brought the newspaper, the Daily Star dated 3 April 1925. Christopher turned the pages very fast. He was looking for the sports section. He stopped at the horse racing. "That's the one! It's the horse I want the bet on at £1000 to win. Bowl Coaster to win."

Christopher was so agitated. He knew he was going to win.

Jimmy looked at the name of the horse. "Are you sure, sir? Bowl Coaster is 300/1 to win. Can I advise Best Mate? The bookmakers give him as 3/1 to win."

"No, trust me Jimmy. Bet on Bowl Coaster."

"I'd better hurry. The race is on in 20 minutes."

"What about the £1,000, Jimmy?"

"Sure, Sir. I will show you where the safe is."

Jimmy and Christopher went to the safe behind the painting in the study.

Jimmy took out £1,000 and closed the safe.

The study was full of shelves of books. Next to the leather chairs facing the marble fireplace, a transparent globe contained bottles of spirits.

Jimmy didn't lose any time. He went out straight away.

Christopher noticed a radio in the study. He had never seen one like it before.

He was very curious.

Impatiently, he started pressing all the buttons. I want to know if I'm lucky.

The radio was on. At last.

"Today ... We are at York races for the Gold Cup 3 miles at 14:45. We have Best Mate at 3/1, Rusty Buster at 7/1, Beau at 8/1, Seal at

10/1, Never Lost at 2/1, and, last, Bowl Coaster at 300/1. What do you think about the race, John?"

"No doubts, grass is firm, Never Lost is on top form and it has strong legs. I bet my house on it!"

"It's the bookmakers' favourite. No chance for Bowl Coaster."

"It's simply out of place amongst these stallions."

"They are ready in the stall and they are off."

"Never Lost is first, second is Seal, third is Best Mate and the pack follows. Last is Bowl Coaster."

"With 2 miles to go, Never Lost is still first followed in second place by Seal and third place is Best Mate. Bowl Coaster is still trailing last."

"Come on Bowl Coaster. Go, go, go, Bowl Coaster."

"Wait a minute. That's incredible! Bowl Coaster is flying. Bowl Coaster is overtaking Rusty Buster in fifth place."

"With one mile to go, Never Lost is still first followed in second place by Seal and Best Mate, but the horse of today is Bowl Coaster, now overtaking Beau in fourth place."

"What a race! Are you excited, John?"

"Yes, Andy. This Bowl Coaster is coasting to win. An outsider is really going to upset the bookmakers."

"With a half-mile to go, Never Lost is head to head with three horses: Seal, Best Mate, and the horse of today, Bowl Coaster."

"Go, go, go, Bowl Coaster. Go Bowl Coaster to win!"

"Last two fences to go. Incredible. Never Lost is slowing down. Probably Never Lost is too tired. It has been leading the entire race."

"Bowl Coaster is leading the group. Second place is between Seal and Best Mate.

Bowl Coaster has a one fence advantage from the second and third places."

"The spectators are delirious. I don't blame them. Who would guess Bowl Coaster to win?"

"Bowl Coaster... Bowl Coaster is the winner followed by a photo finish between Seal and Best Mate and last is Never Lost."

"What do you think, John?"

"It was a thriller, Andy. Congratulations to Bowl Coaster."

"Yes John, congratulations to the horse and jockey."

"Apparently, there is only one winner who bet on Bowl Coaster. His name is...

Christopher Matthews who wins an incredible £300,000."

"Congratulations Christopher Matthews. I don't know if he is lucky or he knew Bowl Coaster was a winner."

"Yes, I won. I broke the curse. We will be lucky forever and ever."

All the noise woke up his dad who ran down the stairs.

"Where are we?"

"It's our house, dad."

"I don't believe you, son. It's impossible. Let's leave before the owner kicks us out."

"Dad trust me. We are the owners, and I broke the curse."

"That's impossible. No one in our family has broken it."

Jimmy returned home with £300,000 and gave it to Christopher. Jimmy confirmed the Matthews were the owners of the massive villa with ten bedrooms, three bathrooms, a kitchen, study, attic, and 100 acres of garden surrounded by trees and flowers and with a swimming pool.

"Hip hip hooray." Sebastian was overjoyed. Sebastian was dancing and jumping in the air. He could not wait to tell his wife and daughter the great news.

He ran up the stairs.

Christopher heard screams of joy. They were dancing too.

Christopher knew his life had turned around and he would never be unlucky again. There was something else Christopher had to do before his life was completely happy.

"Simaco, if you had a wish, what would you like to wish for?"

"Christopher, I would like to be free again, breathing the air, walking on the ground, and having friends like a human being!"

"I wish Simaco would become a real boy."

"Thanks, Christopher!" The coin was all wet. Simaco was weeping for happiness.

A bright light came out of the coin, turning into ashes. The corridor was filled with a white fog.

"Simaco, where are you?"

"I'm here."

"I'm afraid, Simaco."

"Don't be. Soon the fog will vanish."

As soon as Simaco said that, the fog vanished into thin air and a twelve-year-old boy appeared in the corridor.

"Hello, Christopher. What do you think of my new look?"

"You look great, Simaco. How about changing your name?"

"I agree. How about Perry?"

"Hello, Perry."

Perry was a twelve-year-old boy with blonde hair and blue eyes.

His eyes were so blue they seemed to say, I am free. I want to breathe and walk around.

Perry didn't wait any longer. He had been imprisoned in the coin for the past 400 years. The world had changed a lot since he was a genie. He wanted to know and live.

"Thank you, Christopher. You have given me back my life. How can I reward you?"

"You have done so. You made me rich and lucky."

"You made me free, Christopher."

Perry ran out of the front door. Christopher never saw Perry again. He imagined Perry was still traveling around the world, learning, meeting new people, and eating local foods.

Christopher took his life very easily. He got married to Anita in his twenties and they had two children, a boy Andy and a girl Jennifer. He lived for 104 years, happy and lucky.

His luck was transferred from generation to generation.

"That's right my grandson," Anita said.

"You are as lucky as your granddad and your wife and children will be too."

"Granny, I would like to know how you met granddad."

"My dear, that is another story. I will tell you tomorrow. Give your old granny a cuddle."

Little Daniel approached his granny and gave her a warm cuddle.

"Thank you, Daniel."

They both fell asleep and dreamt about Christopher, *The luckiest and happiest man in the world.*

Luke Anderson

L uke Anderson had it all. He had a lucrative job working in his legal firm in Hollywood. He had sex appeal with short blonde hair, deep blue eyes, and a smile that could make women fall at his feet. He came from a rich family. His father, like his grandfather, was a lawyer and they were so successful they never lost a case. They were very clever men, and they knew when their clients were lying. They analysed them and if they felt their clients were liars, they would not take their cases.

Women had chased Luke all his life. They loved him as they found him so down-to-earth and kind. He was not interested in women yet as he was fully concentrating on his education. "There will be plenty of time to settle down.

First I need to become a qualified lawyer then I will find a woman."

As his father and his grandfather, Luke attended the New York University of Law where he excelled with the highest results. During the time Luke spent at the University, he met Clara, in her late twenties, who wanted to become a psychiatrist. She loved helping people solve their personal and emotional problems resulting from traumatic experiences. Clara was gorgeous with curly, blonde, long hair, and a very slim figure. All the male students were so in love with her. Clara was, on the other hand, not interested. She was so absorbed in her studies; she would not engage with anyone.

She loved law and astronomy. On the day Luke and Clara met, she was walking and so distracted with family problems, she crashed against Luke. All her books fell onto the footpath and Clara fell backward.

"Are you OK?" Luke asked with a warm smile.

"Yes, I am sorry it's my fault." Clara blushed.

"Do not worry about it. Give me your hand and I'll help you to stand up."

"Thanks."

Clara's heart was beating very fast. She felt so confused and embarrassed.

Luke felt the same. He did not know what to do or say. He had never had a girlfriend before. Clara had not had a boyfriend either. Their chemistry was strong and profound. They spent so much time together studying law and found out they both loved astronomy.

After graduation, their relationship blossomed so deeply they got married in New York and they moved to Hollywood.

Clara's family was rich as well and her father was an accountant. Clara was preoccupied with her father, Armstrong Carter, during the time of recession as he could lose everything he had. However, her father managed to overcome his financial problems and Clara returned to being more serene.

Clara and Luke bought a mansion house with an electronic gate and a mermaid fountain in front of the house.

Luke was still working as a lawyer even though he did not need to. He had one million dollars in his bank account, but he loved his job too much and wanted to help other hopeless people, who nobody wanted to represent legally. He stopped charging people. He did the work for free. Luke had enough money. He bought several cars for various occasions and states of mind and mood. He had a convertible Ferrari 512 BB, a black Mercedes Benz, a silver Lacetti Chevrolet, and even a limousine for special occasions and VIP entrances.

Clara loved her Ford Fiesta. It was so easy to drive and park.

God blessed their love. It was so pure and everlasting. They had two clever daughters. The oldest was called Jennifer. She was five years old. She wanted to become a pianist. The youngest, who was three years old, was called Jessica.

She wanted to be a successful lawyer like her father.

On the hottest day of summer, Luke was driving his Ferrari. He was feeling the breeze in his hair. It was three o'clock and Luke had finished seeing all his clients and just wanted to spend time with his family in the pool.

All the neighbours were so jealous of Luke. They wanted what he had. His house had one internal swimming pool for winter and an external one at the back of the house, a pool table room, four bedrooms, a large family kitchen, two bathrooms, and two reception rooms.

Luke did not care about the house that much, because the most important thing for him was the people living in it.

Luke pulled the car over in front of the house.

He opened the front door and shouted, "Honey, I am home."

Clara was first to come to welcome him home. She was wearing a bikini.

"Hello darling, how was your day?"

"Wow, you look as beautiful as the day we met."

"Thanks." Clara blushed.

"It was all right, busy as usual. Come and give me some love."

She rushed without a minute's hesitation. She hugged and kissed him.

As soon as Jessica and Jennifer heard their dad's voice, they ran from the back of the house, where they had been swimming, into the hall, and hugged their dad's legs.

"We love you, dad."

"I love you too. All of you are my precious princesses. I would be the happiest and richest man in the world even if I was poor, but I still had all of you in my life."

Luke felt incredibly happy and satisfied.

Ding ding! The alarm clock went off.

It was eight o'clock in the morning.

No, not again. At the best moment, the bloody clock has to go off. It was just getting interesting.

That was the dream and Luke had to go back to reality. In real life, Luke was not married. He had never had a girlfriend. He was not even a lawyer. He was a qualified accountant, but despite his qualifications, he could not get the job he wanted. He had never been lucky. He applied for many jobs, but he only got jobs nobody else applied for. Luke did not care as he needed the money to pay the rent and buy food. He was not living in Hollywood either. He lived in Worcester in England and his house was not a mansion house, as you probably guessed. Trevor, the previous tenant, wanted to make some upgrades to the house without the knowledge of Stewart, the landlord. Trevor had made many holes in the walls.

Some of the neighbours were saying Trevor had a quick temper and Stewart did not sue him because he was too scared of being killed, so he let Trevor off scot-free.

Stewart could not repair the damage as the recession was affecting his business so badly, he could only just manage to keep it afloat.

Luke was all right with it. He was a very tolerant person, and he did not mind about the state of the house.

He had a supposed 'pet' called Frankie. It was a mouse, but it did not belong to Luke. It just helped itself from one of the holes in the house.

It was the only real friend Luke had. He had long conversations with Frankie, but the mouse was not very talkative. It just showed itself if it needed food.

"It is late Frankie. I have to go to work."

Luke had a quick wash, got dressed, and had two jam toasts.

Luke was considered lucky in a way. Many people had lost their jobs. Luke was still working. His job was very physical and mentally tiring. Every day after work he complained of a continuous and acute headache.

He was the only one who was suffering from it and still working. Many of his colleagues were in such pain they called in sick. Some others had been diagnosed with brain tumours derived from the noise of the workplace.

Luke was working on a building site and his duty was to make holes with a pneumatic drill. Even though Luke was wearing a safety helmet and ear defenders, these could not prevent a brain tumour from developing as a result of long exposure to the pneumatic drill.

It seemed the vibration, high sound and long exposure to the pneumatic drill caused damage to the user.

Luke was not afraid of the danger. He had no family and no relatives. His mother died giving birth at the age of 30 and his dad died ten years later when Luke was only ten.

Luke knew that is the destiny of each human being. We are born, we live, and we die. That is our destiny.

He was a very positive person and took his life how it came.

Luke had some other friends on the building site. He liked John and Rob. They had beautiful wives and daughters.

Luke could not spend time with them after work. He was so tired. Sometimes after work, he just wanted to sleep. As soon as he arrived home and saw the bed, he fell onto the mattress and did not wake up until the next morning.

Luke knew something was wrong with him. He was too scared he would lose his job or not get paid by his employer if he found out he was too ill to work.

He kept working no matter what, even when the pain was unbearable.

Today was one of these days; the pain was so acute. Luke felt his head was about to explode. He stopped the pneumatic drill and put his hand on his forehead rubbing it, pretending he was feeling hot.

One minute, Luke was standing tall and proud in his thirties. The next minute he fell like a sack of potatoes onto the gravel. Luke woke up for thirty seconds and heard Rob's voice calling him. His voice echoed in his ears. Luke fell unconscious again into a coma.

The building site doctor ran towards Luke and tried to revive him, but in vain.

After all the failed attempts, without a minute of hesitation, John called the ambulance.

Ten minutes later the ambulance arrived, and the paramedics checked Luke's pulse and eyes.

"Luke, can you hear me?"

Luke did not reply.

"We have to take him to the hospital. He's not responding."

"Can we come?"

"Does he have any family?"

"No, he's only got us."

"OK then, let's go."

The paramedics transported the unconscious Luke in the ambulance followed by John and Rob. The ambulance took ten minutes to reach the hospital.

John and Rob were so preoccupied with Luke's condition.

Luke woke up again to hear the voices of the doctors and nurses around him.

"Where am I?"

"You are in safe hands," the doctor replied.

At the reassuring words, Luke fell asleep again with a serene smile.

Two hours had passed since Luke had fallen unconscious. He was lying in the hospital bed when he woke up. He did not remember what had happened or how he got there. He was resting so peacefully his batteries were charged up.

He could take on the world; he did not feel any pain. Even his acute headache had gone.

"Hello, Luke, my name is Keith. I am your doctor for today."

"Hello, Keith."

"How are you feeling?"

"I'm feeling great."

"Good, I am pleased to hear that. Do you know what happened?"

"No, I was working as usual and then I felt my legs go and all my body switched off. After that, I can't recall a thing."

"Yes, you were in bad shape."

"Now I am feeling great."

"The reason you are feeling great is that I gave you a strong dose of analgesic for your pain."

"I see."

"Do you usually have headaches, Luke?"

"Yes, daily. It is part of the job. Everyone does. I work on a building site and all my colleagues get them."

"I ran some tests on you while you were unconscious… and… I am sorry to tell you I have got some bad news."

Luke knew what was coming. He grabbed the bed linen with his right hand hoping not to hear the B T words.

"Luke, you have a brain tumour."

Luke looked down and with a strange smile replied "It is OK doctor. I will be fine."

The doctor was a bit surprised at his reaction. With warm and sincere words, he replied, "I am sorry we cannot do much for you. If we had known your condition six months ago, we had a fighting chance to defeat the tumour, but at this stage, it is so advanced there is only a very slim chance you will survive. I feel so powerless."

"Do not worry, Keith, I know you have done everything you can to help me."

"We can offer you some analgesics for the pain. I will prescribe them for you and, again, I am sorry I cannot be of more assistance to you."

"Thanks, Keith."

Keith was feeling so down and sad that he could not do more for Luke. He just wanted to save everyone. Sometimes you win some battles, but some other times you lose and that is life.

Luke had to stay in hospital for a week to recover and get used to self-injecting the analgesics.

His job was gone as his employer had already replaced him with a new pneumatic driller who was unaware of the dangers of his new job.

Luke was thrilled he had three months to live and he was looking forward to spending every day in bed, dreaming.

On a few occasions, John and Rob came to see how Luke was doing. They were playing poker and having a beer while Luke was sleeping.

"Luke how are you doing?" Stewart shouted from downstairs.

Luke didn't reply.

"Shall we see if Luke is OK?"

"OK."

John and Rob went upstairs and entered Luke's bedroom. The room smelled unpleasant as if the window had not been opened for a while. Luke was not moving, lying with his face on one side covered by the bed linen.

"I hope you don't mind if I open the window, Luke."

John opened the window. "It's nice fresh air. Can you smell the flowers?"

Again, Luke did not reply.

"Should I check his pulse, John?"

"Why, do you think he's gone?"

Cautiously and slowly, afraid Luke might move, Rob approached the resting body. He was still.

His body was cold and there was no pulse.

"He is dead."

Both Rob and John cried. They were sad no one had said goodbye to Luke before passed away.

Instead, Luke was happy; no alarm clock would interrupt his life again, no headaches would torment him anymore. He would not wake up from his dream of living with his gorgeous wife Clara and his two daughters, Jennifer, and Jessica.

He was the happiest man in the world, living with his precious princesses and he felt his life was now complete.

The Figure Stepped Out of a Doorway

The figure stepped out of a doorway in The Shambles. It was tall, wearing a black coat. It was a man with bristled white hair and pale freckled pink skin. He looked at his hands. They were covered in spattered blood.

It was not his blood. How did this happen? Why am I here? He was looking disoriented and trying to reconstruct all the events before he found himself in The Shambles.

Scratching his head, blood was pouring down his face, but he could not figure it out. This blood-stained me. I need to get rid of it. He was in a panic. Without thinking, he was rubbing his hands on the black coat, ruining the exquisite wool fabric. His coat seemed to have witnessed manslaughter.

What a pellock. I have made it worse. My coat is screaming "he did it". I got time. If I turn my coat inside out, no one will ever know. The Shambles was deserted, it was a cold winter night and the York Minster cathedral clock had struck midnight.

The strange man reversed his coat and a divine intervention made the rain pour down, soaking him from head to toe, washing off the shameful blood.

He sighed deeply and walked on with a smile on his face. *No one will ever know what I have done. If I knew what I did.* A passer-by stared at a strange man wearing a reversed coat, smiling, and whistling in the pouring rain. He was already well known as an insane man who acted very weirdly. His name was Sebastian Madlove. He had led a normal life without showing any signs of insanity until he fell in love with a gold-digger wife who took his house, money, and common sense, leaving him penniless and broken-hearted. Sebastian started to behave antisocially and get in trouble with the police. He had been caught stealing from a supermarket or peeing against the wall. Then his behaviour escalated into assaulting people without a reason. Sebastian was not a bad man.

In his mind, he could see the world was against him. They wanted to hurt him.

There was a voice in his head which was telling him what to do and Sebastian was following it to the letter. He had lucid moments where no one could distinguish him from an individual with no mental problems.

Sebastian returned home and as soon as he opened the door, a sickening stench welcomed him into his house. It was pitch black. Sebastian had a flashback.

He stood still in the corridor leading to the kitchen. He remembered. Now I remember. It was a sad memory. Two hours earlier he was in the kitchen making a cup of tea when someone knocked at his door. It was his neighbour, the beautiful Michelle. "Hi Sebastian, can I have some sugar? I am making a cake and I thought you could help me."

"Yes, of course, Michelle, come in."

"Thanks, you're a star."

They walked to the kitchen. The voice was whispering to Sebastian. "She is a bitch; she is telling all your neighbours you are mental."

Stop, you are a liar. She is not like the others.

"Have I ever lied to you?"

No, not ever, smiling at Michelle.

"Listen to me. Offer her a slice of the lemon cake and stab her. If you don't do it, I will pester you all night."

OK, I will do it, but shut up.

"Would you like a slice of lemon cake, Michelle?"

"I need to be careful, Sebastian, cakes make me fat."

"Trust me, Michelle; this lemon cake is fat-free."

"OK, if you insist. I will have a small piece."

Sebastian took a butcher's knife from the draw and sliced the cake.

"This is the moment; she is not looking."

Michelle was admiring the pottery in the cupboard.

Sebastian ran towards her and stabbed her in her back twice. Her blood spattered onto his hands. She turned around and shouted, "Why have you stabbed me, Sebastian?" before falling on the tiled kitchen floor.

"Well done, Sebastian, you see you can do anything when you put your mind to it."

"What have I done?" I fancied Michelle. She was the only person who cared about me and now I have killed her.

"Run Sebastian do not come back."

He took his wool coat and ran out of the door.

"Why are you back?" the voice screamed in his head.

"I have to do this. I cannot run forever."

He went to the phone, dialled 999, and confessed his crime. The police arrived ten minutes later. Sebastian was waiting in the living room, drinking a cup of tea.

He never denied he had stabbed Michelle. Despite the fact the voice was whispering lie after lie, Sebastian decided to block the voice in his head and took responsibility for his actions. He spent ten years in prison. He was happy. *I won't hurt anyone anymore and everyone is safe*, looking outside through the bars of his Hull prison cell.

There Must Be More Money

There must be more money. There must be more money, the walls were whispering. On cold days the whispers sounded louder. Nicholas Roberts hated these moments. He was attempting to block them by covering his ears with his filthy hands, staring at the spider's web in the high corner of the ceiling of his bedroom. He welcomed the distraction, hoping to silence the walls. He was so fascinated by the spider's engineering; he did not expect the walls to raise the volume of their tone.

There must be more money.

Nicholas, slightly frightened and shaken, jumped up from his old torn fabric mattress revealing several emerging coiled springs. His bedroom was furnished with a three-legged wooden chair leaning against the black mouldy wall, and a torn and worn rug covered by dead ants and beetles.

Nicholas was reflecting on how his life had turned out and he felt embarrassed.

He had been begging in the street for the past two years. He had never been poor before. He remembered how his hands were pink and clean and now they were scruffy and dirty. How he loved shaving his face. Now a full reddish beard, covered by breadcrumbs from the night before, hid the smooth Irish skin.

A delightful memory surface in his mind. His cheeks brightened with pleasure at the reminiscence of sitting on a computer chair staring at a monitor, inputting data into internal computer software. His job involved daily drowsy tedious repetitive tasks, but Nicholas loved it. He was earning ten pounds an hour. The best day of the week was Friday. His blue eyes were watering with ecstasy.

Logging in his bank account at the ATM in the main street of Leeds, gazing at the screen he leaped in the air with joy. Three hundred pounds had been deposited in his penniless bank account. Now that surreal reality sounded an illusion. Being brought back to normality had a knock-on effect on self-confidence.

Faultless of losing his temporary contract, he acquired a new employer "The government" and a new payment term of seventy-eight pounds a week, just enough to cover the rent of a dilapidated flat.

Nicholas did not have much choice. Begging was the only solution for keeping starvation at bay as times were tough. Inflation had contributed to the rise in food prices and the poor were the first to struggle to cope. On rainy, snowy, or sunny days, Nicholas sat on cold stones, holding a piece of paper:

"Your spare change can feed me today, please help this unfortunate man."

He felt overwhelmed by the generosity of passers-by and some women were so moved by his condition, tears rolled down their pink cheeks. Every coin dropped by strangers into his wool hat full of holes lifted his heart. His hat was in mint condition when he bought it. He blamed the mice living in his flat. These mice had caused so much damage to his clothes. They chewed the fabric of his hat, socks, and shirts leaving circular holes in the process. Nicholas was not a vindictive man. He forgave the mice and fate for being so cruel to him. His Irish spirit kept him optimistic, even in adversity.

It was a cold rainy day. Nicholas was sitting on a concrete floor in Leeds city centre, soaked and frozen, staring at his shoes and holding the piece of paper, unaware the day would change his life forever. A man approached him wearing an expensive coat, leather gloves, and an Irish hat.

"It is you, isn't it? It is Nicholas, my lost nephew. I have been traveling all over the world looking for you and now I have found you."

Nicholas was perplexed and confused. In his state of mind and food deprivation, he raised his eyes. The image of the man talking blurred. He felt a mirage was in front of him. The stranger's voice awoke a

102

great memory. He remembered the time he had spent in Ireland with his uncle.

"Uncle Tom, is it you? Am I dreaming?"

"You are not dreaming, Nicholas. It is me. Let me help you to get up," Tom said, offering his hand.

"Thank you, uncle." Tears rolled down Nicholas's skinny face.

Nicholas took his uncle to his dilapidated flat and explained what had happened to his life. Tom was listening to every single word. He cried several times, moved by his nephew's condition.

"Today your life is going to change for the better."

"What do you mean uncle?"

"You are coming with me back to Ireland. You are going to work for me in my pub."

At the thought of working again, Nicholas was excited and felt valued as a human being.

"Yes, sure uncle. I will do anything to move away from this depressing flat."

"We both agree. Tomorrow we will take a flight back to Ireland and tonight you will stay at my five-star hotel. You will get properly fed, dressed, and washed."

"Thank you, uncle. I'm speechless."

"You were lost, and I found you."

The next day Nicholas and Tom flew back to Ireland. Nicholas never experienced poverty again. He became an extremely healthy man and founded a charity for helping the less fortunate. He spent all his life changing the lives of others as he could not bear watching people struggle anymore.

The Darkness and the Light

I t had been raining all day. The significance of the rain had some meaning for me.

I felt a therapeutic treatment of depression and stress. I was telling myself, but the rain had other intentions. I knew something was not right. I had been staring at it for a while. I had been pulled into its mystical and obscure magical power. I felt overpowered by it. I was so immersed; I had lost all consciousness of time.

In this relaxed state of mind, my thoughts were aiming at planning my day ahead, but the rain had won the battle. I was hypnotized. My weak mind was moulded by the liquid drops falling from the dark clouds.

I was sitting in my armchair, inert, stony, deprived of my humanity and emotions.

My living room and its contents were shadowed by darkness, disconnecting all the colours. They regained their original state temporarily when forked lightning struck in the distance.

The silence and darkness claimed victory once again. The room was chilled and unwelcoming. A cold breeze circulated in the most popular room of the house where joy had been the centre of the family life, day and night. Now fear and terror had overwhelmed the remote pleasant memories.

The television, focal point for entertainment, giving my family laughter and fun, was powerless and broken, occupying wasted space.

The lamp next to the TV set, a saviour of dark nights, was lifeless ready to join the list of unwanted items for charity.

Even the boiler could not escape this negative overwhelming powerful atmosphere. Its last flame had vanished. The last hope for warmth, for comfort, for happiness, for sanity had been taken away. The house seemed to say 'you enter at your own risk. You have been warned'.

Lucy, my wife, was not aware of the danger. She turned the key and entered.

She felt a shiver down her arms. She rubbed herself, giving herself confidence.

She felt something was wrong. The house had never been so chilled and unwelcoming. "Again, another blackout," she shouted. Her voice resounded loud and echoed in each room. "Andrew are you there?" I did not reply. I was inert, lifeless like the house. "This is not funny. I am scared Andrew. Please say something."

Her pleading had no effect. "I understand. Like always I have got to save the day."

In the darkness, Lucy stumbled on furniture, using her hands for guidance and, walking slowly, she managed to go to the kitchen. "Listen, mister, when I have sorted this out, you will be severely punished."

Lucy went through the kitchen cupboard until she found what she was looking for. "Finally, I've got it." She lit a white candle. The kitchen came back to life.

The devices became alive again. The fridge and microwave gained the power which previously had been absorbed.

Her focus was now on the living room. As soon as she entered, the darkness gradually receded back to normality. The television and the lamp lit again.

The boiler flame came back to life, starting to heat up each room. But I was unconscious, unable to move or talk until Lucy touched my arm. My stony body was shattered into millions of pieces reclaiming my humanity and ability of movement and speech.

I was delighted to see the white candle and the yellow flame. I knew the evil spell was broken by my white-witch wife.

"Are you OK, Andrew? You scared me tonight," she said, putting her arms around my warm body.

"Yes, I am darling. I do not know what happened, but I am OK now. I love you, darling."

The Last 5 Minutes

Five minutes seemed like longevity, but Thomas wished he had more time.

He had been unconscious for over one hour. His last memory was yesterday.

He was going to the car park when he noticed a white van. As soon as he approached the van, two men wearing black clothes and balaclavas opened its sliding door. It happened so fast. They grabbed Thomas and one of the men put a tissue impregnated with anaesthetic on his face. He tried to resist the drug and escape from the danger, but the drug was so intense his body collapsed.

Now he found himself strapped to a bomb which was going to explode in five minutes. His hands were handcuffed round the back of a concrete pilaster. A tight rope was blocking his mouth impeding any call for help. He was in a deserted car park.

Who is behind this crime? Why am I here? I do not have any enemies. Could I have been a victim of mistaken identity? Thomas was very confused.

He was a normal man. He and his parents were middle-class workers. They had just enough money to pay their bills. It is not worth asking for a ransom for me.

Thomas understood he had been in the wrong place at the wrong time. Tears rolled down his face and his reddish beard, knowing his life was ending very soon. The bomb was ticking the last five minutes of his life and he could not do anything to change that. He started to remember all the best memories of his life.

Only one memory emerged, vivid and intense. It was the day when he met Lisa and he fell in love. He had been single for the past eight years.

His last girlfriend broke his heart, dumping him on the same day that his sister died in a car accident.

His life seemed to change for the better since he and Lisa had become a couple.

He was blessed every single day. He was telling everyone how lucky he was. *Lisa has got blonde curly hair and green eyes. Her smile is so beautiful and warm.* What Thomas did not know was that Lisa had a jealous ex-boyfriend called Jack, who was very possessive and controlling. Her ex did not want anyone to steal his woman. Jack was also a bad man involved in crimes. Lisa was tired of this bad relationship and wanted out. She had dumped Jack. Jack started stalking her and, from one of his friends, he discovered Lisa was dating Thomas. Jack was fuming and organized a vindictive plan to punish Thomas.

In his last two minutes, Thomas was praying to God. Oh God, I forgive these two men who handcuffed me and strapped me to this bomb. I ask your forgiveness for all the sins I have done in my life. Please tell Lisa I love her with all my heart.

Thomas closed his eyes and was preparing himself to die when he heard some voices. Two bomb experts disarmed the ticking explosive and a police officer freed Thomas.

Half an hour earlier, the guard of the car park had noticed Thomas and called the police. The guard also described two men driving a white van. Later that evening Jack and his accomplice were arrested for kidnapping and attempted murder.

They spent 10 years in prison while Thomas and Lisa got married and had a beautiful son.

Haunted?

T homas heard metallic and disturbing noises in the attic. He was standing on the landing.

The noises were clear light footsteps on a bare wooden floor. He was puzzled and disturbed. He had lived alone for many years in his deceased father's mansion and no odd noise had ever been reported to him since he had moved in.

"Come out or I call the police," his intimidating voice echoed in the empty house.

The noises stopped briefly. Thomas looked even more perplexed.

He pinched himself and slapped his face with force. "Ouch!"

The noises returned with vengeance.

Someone or something was stamping loudly on the floor. It was upsetting and sickening. Thomas had goosebumps.

With a deep breath, he took courage. "Right, I am coming up. You are in serious trouble when I get my hands on you!"

He walked nervously up the squeaky stairs leading to the attic.

Sssh, I'm making too much noise. Great! I'm losing the element of surprise.

His knees were shaking. His hands were trembling as they moved up the handrail.

He turned the rustic knob and the squeaky door opened wide.

The attic was stuffy, dark, and nauseous. It reminded him of the smell of a decomposed carcass. Thomas could hardly see the shape of a sofa and chairs covered by white bedsheets lit by rays of sunshine coming through holes in the ceiling and walls. At the far end of the attic, an old chest of drawers was close to the wall.

There was no sign of any activity.

"It is better for you to show up. You are already in so much trouble."

His words echoed in the empty and lifeless room.

"OK, then."

Without warning, the door slammed in front of his petrified eyes, making him jump. The noises came back again even louder than before. Something was jumping up and down on the wooden floor, making the ceiling plaster fall off.

Thomas could make out another noise. It sounded like the violent continuous opening and closing of a draw.

He assumed it was the chest of drawers. He tried to investigate what was happening, but now the door was shut, hiding the dark secret.

Great. My house is haunted.

Does the ghost know is it illegal to move in without a tenancy agreement?

Who could it be?

It cannot be my dad as he died peacefully. No other people have been murdered or died mysteriously in the history of the house.

Thomas was scared and shaking. He took his phone from his pocket, dialling the emergency service. There was no signal.

Without thinking, he ran towards the stairs leading to the ground floor, but the stairs had vanished.

Feeling like an animal in a cage without a way out, Thomas started to shout:

"Someone, please help me. Someone, please help me. I don't want to die." He was crying and begging in desperation.

"Wake up Thomas, you are scaring me. Wake up Thomas." His wife Kim was shaking him, not sure what to do next to help her husband in distress.

Thomas woke up and he was pleased to see her. He was not in his father's house and it had all been a nightmare.

He was in a flat cottage being stared at by his wife with her fists on her waist and her arms akimbo.

"Sorry dear. I had a terrible dream."

"I know you did. You have been sleepwalking again!"

Other Publications

The author Paolo Debernardi is going to publish these forthcoming books and in the following pages there is a description of what to expect:

"Idyllic paths Sentieri Idillici" A book of Italian poetry and proverbs with an English translation.

"Angelic Dreams" His first English poetry book.

"Timothy Divine and his adventures" His first English novel.

"Dr Victor Slater and the World" His second English novel.

"Idyllic Paths Sentieri Idillici"

"Idyllic Paths" is not just a collection of poetry and maxims in Italian, with reviews and English translations, but is also a journey in which my emotions and daily life emerge and seek to communicate my suffering, hopes, and quest for happiness in a language accessible to everyone.

In writing my compositions, I have managed to find one of my dimensions and partially satisfied that quest for happiness. Through my words, I collect everything around me reproducing it in the same way.

In my biographical compositions, themes and styles vary from youth to maturity.

Poetry dedicated to nature, the seasons and places follows poetry dedicated to Italian television presenters, the love for Miriana Trevisan, and the friendship of Rosario Fiorello and Stefano Gallarini and to my sad life where suffering, paternal violence, and the lack of affection from my family emerge in a dominant way.

Continuing to write, I realized that meter was suppressing my inspiration and originality.

Without obstacles, new poems sprang up with many varied themes, for example, the sea, dawn, nature, the UFO, and love. Through my poetry, I am sending a message to my contemporaries and future generations to enjoy and protect what surrounds us and to help our neighbours.

Thank you for the compliment you are paying me through the selection of this volume.

I hope that you like and enjoy reading "Idyllic Paths" and that you will read my future publications.

Paolo Debernardi (The Author)

"Angelic Dreams"

The most striking element of these poems is the imaginative way in which the language is used. They illustrate very clearly the advantages of creating poetry in a foreign language, for in this situation one is not fettered by some of the basic rules that so often inhibit those writing in their mother tongue.

In this book you will find a great sensitivity to the sound of the language, most especially in such poems as "Fireworks" and "I belong everywhere". Here the combination of sound and rhythm greatly enhances the imagery.

One has the impression of traveling through a poetic landscape in which one looks at everything with new eyes. The poems "England" and "Soap bubbles" are examples of this "fresh" vision.

However, by far the most moving aspect of this work is that it portrays a young person on the very threshold of life, for these verses exude all the joy, the pain, and the vulnerability of youth. They show with considerable eloquence that special moment in life when one is aware of so many possibilities, which seem to be almost within one's grasp.

The hopes and the pain of almost, but not quite, realizing one's dreams are all to be found in this collection of poems.

Young readers will have no difficulty in identifying with the feelings and imagery they will find here, whilst those who are no longer in their first youth will recapture the emotions of that unique time in their lives.

David Sanderson (English teacher)

"Timothy Divine and His Adventures"

"Timothy Divine and his Adventures" is the first English novel, which tells the story of Timothy Divine, a 10-year-old boy exploring new worlds in his rocket ship and interacting with his grandfather Jo and his friends.

The novel has a lot of funny and emotional moments which I am sure the reader will enjoy and share with family and friends.

"Dr Victor Slater and the World"

"Dr Victor Slater and the World" is the second English novel, in which the author tells how Dr Victor Slater and humanoid dinosaurs worked together in protecting Earth from the invasion of an evil alien race, Y42.

In this novel, the reader will come across a love triangle, comedy, and drama.

Autobiography

Paolo Debernardi was born on 3 July 1973 in Casale Monferrato (province of Alessandria) in Piedmont but lived with his family in Mortara (province of

Pavia, southwest of Milan) in Lombardy until 1997.

In June of that year, he moved to Bishopthorpe and from there to York in England in the United Kingdom, where he lived until March 2001.

Because of his work, he moved to Worcester where he lived until July 2002 and in August of the same year, he decided to transfer to Glasgow in Scotland until 2006.

He moved back to York from 2006 until 2009.

From a small child, he demonstrated his success, winning various awards in the Youth Games in Mortara, in the painting and sports competitions.

A symbolic collection of medals took him to the Collegio San Carlo di Borgo San Martino as an accountant and commercial expert and here he discovered his greatest loves: being a football manager helping his teams win several trophies, and poetry, through studying the French symbolists Charles Baudelaire and

Arthur Rimbaud.

These two great writers aroused a passion in Paolo Debernardi and this prompted him to write innumerable poetic biographies, maxims, and dedications embracing different themes and styles to the point where they were put into a collection, together with reviews from university lecturers and writers and the drawings of Salvatore Sepe, in his first book, now out of print, entitled

"Saranno state le onde del mare d'inverno ..." 1 published by Edizioni Nuove Proposte U.A.O.C., (Union for Artists and Cultural workers) in Marigliano, Naples, Italy, in November 1996.

Through his poetry, *Paolo Debernardi* has appeared in many Italian anthologies, having taken part in and won many prizes in several poetry competitions published in his native country.

He is also known in Germany and Australia at a local level and on the website entitled "www.storymania.com".

With his move to England and change in mentality, *Paolo Debernardi* has put aside Italian literature to pursue an immense challenge, albeit a more satisfying one, of writing poetry and short stories in English because English is a language spoken and recognized throughout the world.

Notwithstanding any difficulties, his determination and inspiration have enabled *Paolo Debernardi* to write English poems and short stories to such a degree of success that he came second in an English poetry competition published by the White Tower Writers Association in Doncaster, England, and first in a poetry competition published in the town of Bova Marina, Italy.

His English poems have also appeared in several anthologies in Italy, Australia, Germany, England, Switzerland, and Brazil and on the web page "www.storymania.com".

In 2000, *Paolo Debernardi* started to write English short stories and one entitled "They always come back" was published by the White Tower Writers Association in the review entitled "The Partial Eclipse".

The three short stories entitled "They always come back", "Waiting" and "Delta Centauri" are also included on the web page "www.storymania.com".

Besides writing this volume, in the future, *Paolo Debernardi* will publish a volume of English poetry with reviews, drawings, and colour photographs, entitled *"Angelic Dreams"*, and a volume of Italian poetry and proverbs with English translations entitled *"Idyllic Paths Sentieri Idillici"*. He also plans his first English novel, *"Timothy*

Divine and his Adventures", and a second English novel, "*Dr Victor Slater and the World*" published by Debernardi Publishing.

In 2009, *Paolo Debernardi* published his first English short-story book entitled "*The Twelve Wonders*", which is available as a paperback and an e-book. This book was published by AuthorHouse and it is sold in 26 countries.

In 2011, *Paolo Debernardi* appeared on *So You Think You Can Dance*, broadcast on BBC1, performing in front of the judges Nigel Lythgoe, Arlene Phillips, Louise Redknapp, and Sisco Gomez, and meeting Cat Deeley.

In 2012, *Paolo Debernardi* appeared in *Got to Dance*, broadcast by Sky One, performing in front of the judges Ashley Banjo, Adam Garcia, and Kimberly Wyatt.

In 2013, *Paolo Debernardi* appeared in *The Harry Hill Movie* as an extra.

In 2014, *Paolo Debernardi* appeared as an extra in *Vivid Colour* and *Prime Contact*, where his name appeared in the credits.

In 2015, *Paolo Debernardi* appeared as an extra in *Please next*, where he had a non-speaking part and his name appeared in the credits, and as an extra in *Scott & Sydd*.

In 2016, *Paolo Debernardi* appeared as an extra in *Carthasys*, where his name is in the credits, and in *Britain's Got Talent*. However, his audition was not broadcast by ITV1. He met *Ant and Dec, Simon Cowell, Amanda Holden, Alesha Dixon, David Walliams,* and *Stephen Mulhern.*

In 2018, *Paolo Debernardi* was an extra in *Kings* and *Queens*.

In 2019, *Paolo Debernardi* was in the community ensemble as Mr. Lipari in the play *A view from the bridge by Arthur Miller in the York Theatre Royal* from 20 September until 12 October and on 15 October he performed in a dance group. In the same year, *Paolo Debernardi* appeared in a short film *Break Time* as the main actor, Mr. Davis.

Paolo Debernardi has met many famous people including Ronnie O'Sullivan, Jimmy White, John Virgo, Suggs, Andy Parsons, Nikki

Sanderson, Harry Hill, Sarah Jayne Dunn, Rupert Hill, and many more.

Please go to the following link for competitions, book releases, and latest updates of Paolo Debernardi's TV, film, and theatre appearances:

https://forms.aweber.com/form/11/351188711.htm

Lightning Source UK Ltd.
Milton Keynes UK
UKHW012109080822
407014UK00001B/92

9 781914 078101